SUPERBIKES

ROAD MACHINES OF THE '60s, '70s, '80s and '90s

SUPERBIKES

ROAD MACHINES OF THE '60s, '70s, '80s and '90s

Roland Brown

CHARTWELL
BOOKS, INC.

Published by
CHARTWELL BOOKS, INC.
A Division of BOOK SALES, INC.
110 Enterprise Avenue
Secaucus, New Jersey 07094

Produced by
Brompton Books Corp.
15 Sherwood Place
Greenwich, CT 06830

ISBN 1-55521-860-1

Printed in Italy

Page 1: The beautiful lines of
the Buell RS1200, a stylish
and innovative machine.

Pages 2-3: The Kawasaki
ZXR750 captured taking a
corner.

These pages: The Magni
Sfida, capable of a top speed
of 140mph.

Contents

INTRODUCTION

Right: The power and the glory. MV Agusta's mighty four-cylinder 750S engine of the Seventies was developed from the Italian firm's all-conquering racing machines.

Right: Ducati's watercooled, eight-valve 851 V-twin heralded a new era for the once-troubled Bologna factory, laying the foundation for huge road and track success in the Nineties.

Below right: Suzuki's GSX-R750 race-replica dominated the late Eighties and is still popular now, thanks to its thrilling blend of power, light weight and singleminded sporting intent.

'Super' is a word that is too often used to describe the mediocre, but it rings true when put in front of 'bike' to give superbike. Since the Seventies, when the term became popular, superbike has been used to define a select band of machines dedicated to high technology, high performance and the high excitement of biking at the redline. No other road-going vehicle has come close to providing the exhilaration that superbike riders have enjoyed over the years. The top bikes' awesome power-to-weight ratios give acceleration that makes even the best contemporary sportscars seem sluggish. Honda's CB750 ruled the roads in its day, and the modern CBR900RR FireBlade screams from 0 to 60 mph in 2.5 seconds – twice as fast as a Lamborghini.

On a superbike you're out there in the elements, too, not cosseted behind steel and glass. The wind tears at your shoulders. Your boots, perhaps even the knees of your leathers, touch asphalt through the bends. You feel the sun or the rain – and if you're lucky, you smell the diesel on the road up ahead before it tips you off. Danger is never far away on a superbike, and for many riders that's part of the thrill. These sensations are not remotely new, because superbikes existed long before the term was coined. You could argue that the first ever motorbike, a 264cc single built by German engineer Gottlieb Daimler in 1885, was pretty 'super' itself. Only two years later the British firm Holden produced a bike with four cylinders and a capacity of 1047cc.

By the early years of this century, European manufacturers such as Scott and FN were competing with American firms Indian and Henderson to build singles, fours and big-bore V-twins. Those machines must have provided serious excitement in the days of unmade roads, bicycle-style tires and no suspension – not to mention the absence of crash-helmets and leathers. The definitive early roadster was Britain's Brough Superior, a thundering V-twin that was capable of a genuine 100 mph in the Thirties. In subsequent years many of the best bikes were 500cc single machines mimicking the trend in road-racing like the Manx Norton, BSA Gold Star and Velocette Venom.

In the Forties and Fifties, the dominant British manufacturers' best-loved design was the parallel twin. Most successful were Triumph's 500cc Speed Twin and its legendary derivative, the Bonneville, and Norton's Dominator, which grew into the famous Commando. More impressive still was the Vincent Black Shadow, a powerful and hugely expensive 998cc V-twin with a top speed of over 120 mph.

These are the bikes that set the scene for the machines covered in the following pages. While the British manufacturers stagnated in the Sixties, the Japanese were waiting in the wings refining their small bikes in preparation to take over the main event. They arrived at full throttle in the Seventies, sparking a spirited response from older manufacturers, particularly those in Italy. The result was a wide variety of stunning bikes displaying spiraling sophistication and performance. There's that word performance again. More than anything else, that's what all of the superbikes in this book are about.

TRIUMPH TRIDENT 750

The three-cylinder Trident epitomized motorcycling's shift of power in the late Sixties away from old-style British parallel twins toward the new world of Japanese fours. Launched in 1968, the Trident was fast, fine-handling and arguably the first ever superbike. But it lacked the refinement, the reliability and the sheer glamor of Honda's CB750, which arrived a year later to take the wind out of the British bike's sails – and its sales.

Typically, BSA Triumph (formed by a merger between the two companies) did not capitalize quickly enough on the three-cylinder format, which had been mooted by engineers Bert Hopwood and Doug Hele several years earlier. By the time the bike was put into production, its pushrod valve operation, drum brakes and lack of electric start were on the verge of becoming old fashioned. The 60bhp triple, however, was certainly no slouch. The factory initially produced two separate models, the Triumph Trident T150 and the BSA Rocket-3, which were near-identical apart from the Rocket-3's angled-forward engine. Both were capable of close to 120mph, with acceleration to match and a thrillingly high-pitched exhaust wail.

Triples dominated the racetracks in the early Seventies. The Meriden factory's bikes finished first, second and third at Daytona in 1971 (Dick Mann winning, as he had the year before on a Honda), and in the following seasons notched up dozens of victories at the hands of riders such as John Cooper, Ray Pickrell and Percy Tait. The most famous triple was the production racer nicknamed 'Slippery Sam,' which won consecutive Isle of Man TTs from 1971 to 1975.

Roadster development did not always benefit from the factory's racing commitments, and was further hampered by the firm's growing financial problems. One variation, the X-75 Hurricane, was a custom bike with high bars, a sleek one-piece seat-tank unit and three mufflers aligned up its right side. Stylish, yes – but expensive, impractical and years ahead of its time in 1973.

The Trident's first serious revision did not come until 1975 with the T160, which combined handsome new looks of its own with overdue refinements such as an electric start and disc brakes. The 125mph T160 was the definitive British superbike, but it still lacked the speed and sophistication of the best of the current Japanese opposition. And, to make matters worse, it could do nothing to reverse Triumph's headlong slide toward financial disaster.

TRIUMPH TRIDENT T150 (1968)

Engine	Aircooled 6-valve pushrod transverse triple
Capacity	740cc
Claimed power	60bhp at 7250rpm
Weight	209kg (460lbs) dry
Top speed	118mph (188km/h)
Standing quarter-mile	13sec/100mph (160km/h)

Right: Despite the later T160 Trident's handsome looks and thrilling performance, the triple could do nothing to prevent Triumph's financial decline.

Below right: Adding an electric starter gave the T160 Trident's motor a new lease of life without losing its distinctive three-cylinder character or exhaust note.

Below: The original T150 Trident, with its angular styling and distinctive 'raygun' silencers, was a fast, fine-handling machine but lacked the CB750's refined feel.

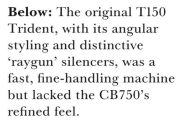

HONDA CB750

Honda's 750-four was the original superbike; the machine that redefined the limits of motorcycle performance almost overnight. Actually born in the Sixties – it was unveiled at the Tokyo Show in October 1968, and released in limited numbers the following year – the CB750 dominated the early Seventies and had a huge influence on the machines that followed it. Until the arrival of the Honda, with its broad bank of aircooled cylinders and four shining mufflers, mass-produced fours simply did not exist. The CB750 changed all that and went further, combining its basic appeal with a competitive price that included refinements such as a disc front brake and electric starter.

It was the Honda's engine that created all the impact. The angled-forward 736cc unit's design used many lessons learnt during Honda's days of racing multi-cylinder machines in the Sixties, although the roadster relied on a single overhead camshaft and two valves per cylinder, in contrast to the racers with their twin cams and four valves per pot. The CB750's output of 67bhp was mighty impressive at the time, though, as were the smoothness and reliability with which it was delivered. The CB was designed as an all-rounder, with a view to sales in the important American market, but was good for over 120mph despite its high, wide handlebars.

Handling, however, was only adequate, with the flex-prone steel frame and harsh suspension later coming in for criticism. But in the excitement of the CB's arrival few riders were put off by that – especially after veteran Dick Mann had proved the four's sporting potential by winning at Daytona in 1970. Honda sat on their laurels a little, barely updating the 750 even when Kawasaki launched the faster 900cc Z1 four years later. In fact, the CB was detuned slightly over the years to reduce emissions. When Honda finally revamped it in 1976 with the so-called Super Sports CB750F – complete with flat handlebars, bright yellow paint and a four-into-one exhaust – the new bike's top speed was only 115mph.

The single-cam CB750 soldiered on for a full decade, finally being replaced by the 16-valve CB750K – a disastrous bike that combined poor handling with a series of mechanical problems. But the memory of that first great superbike remains with the faithful.

HONDA CB750 (1969)

Engine	Aircooled 8-valve SOHC transverse four
Capacity	736cc
Claimed power	67bhp at 8000rpm
Weight	218kg (480lbs) dry
Top speed	125mph (200km/h)
Standing quarter-mile	13.5sec/100mph (160km/h)

Left: The original CB750's unprecedented combination of power, reliability and sophistication led to the term 'superbike' being coined in its honor.

Inset: This immaculate CB750 was photographed for Honda's brochures when new. It still runs perfectly and turns plenty of heads, over 20 years later.

KAWASAKI Z1

If one machine summed up the spirit of Seventies superbiking, it was Kawasaki's Z1, which burst on to the scene in 1973 and dominated the decade with a performance that put it streets ahead – often literally – of the opposition. The first big 'Zed' was a landmark motorcycle, raising the speed stakes to new heights and establishing a reputation for brute power and reliability that Kawasaki has retained to this day.

The Z1's early story is one of triumph over near disaster. In the fall of 1968, Kawasaki's engineers were dismayed when, with their own plans for a radical four-cylinder 750 well advanced, they were suddenly confronted by Honda's CB750. Kawasaki considered scrapping their project, code-named 'New York Steak' – but, instead, they learnt all they could from the Honda, enlarged their own twin-camshaft engine to 903cc, and returned four years later with the Z1.

The wait and the extra work were worthwhile, because the Kawasaki was a better bike in almost every way. Its big motor put out 82bhp – 15bhp more than the single-cam Honda, and enough to give a top speed of 130mph. It was smooth, it was tractable and it was almost unburstable. Tuners and racers adopted it in droves, and Z1-based bikes were soon competing successfully at every level from club-racing to the international endurance events.

But there was much more to the Z1 than simply an engine. The bike's rounded styling was striking, its handling was reasonable (though when pushed hard the Kawa could get seriously out of shape), and it was even fairly comfortable despite the high handlebars. The inescapable conclusion when comparing CB750 with Z1 was: 'The King is dead. Long live the King.' Such was the performance of the Kawasaki

Above: It looked right and it was right. The Z1 matched slick styling with a 903cc twin-cam engine whose smoothness, strength and 82bhp output gave the Z1 top performance.

Right: Handling was respectable by early-Seventies standards, but the Z1's chassis combination of simple frame, skinny forks and single disc ensured that a rider had to be brave.

that it needed virtually no changes to remain on top when it became the Z900 in 1976; it merely gained a second front disc brake and slightly firmer suspension. A year later came the Z1000, its motor bored out to 1015cc to give even more low-rev smoothness and punch.

The following years saw the big 'Zed' in a variety of guises: cafe-racer Z1-R, shaft-drive Z1000ST tourer, and later the fiery red GPz1100 sportster. All were good bikes.

KAWASAKI Z1 (1973)

Engine	Aircooled 8-valve DOHC transverse four
Capacity	903cc
Claimed power	82bhp at 8500rpm
Weight	230kg (506lbs) dry
Top speed	130mph (208km/h)
Standing quarter-mile	12.5sec/110mph (176km/h)

KAWASAKI 750 H2

Take a ride on Kawasaki's 750 H2 now, in these times of safety-consciousness and environmental awareness, and the legendary two-stroke triple would seem like a bike from another planet. Fast, loud, smoky, vibratory, thirsty and evil-handling, the H2 and its predecessor the Mach IV were outrageously anti-social even by the somewhat lax standards of the early Seventies.

Kawasaki pulled no punches in setting out to establish the snarling stroker's performance credentials. The first paragraph of their brochure read: 'The Kawasaki 750 Mach IV has only one purpose in life: to give you the most exciting and exhilarating performance. It's so quick it demands the razor-sharp reactions of an experienced rider. It's a machine you must take seriously.'

They weren't joking. The original aircooled 748cc motor put out 74bhp, which was enough to send the triple screaming to 120mph while spewing clouds of oily blue smoke from its exhausts. Light weight and a short wheelbase meant fearsome acceleration and plenty of wheelies. Awful fuel consumption – around 22mpg was common – necessitated frequent fill-ups, but the upright riding position and tingling engine vibration meant the rider was often relieved to stop. And sometimes relieved to be alive, for the triple's handling was even more notorious than its engine performance. The Mach IV, in particular, was distinctly lively, combining a none-too-strong frame with crude suspension with the result that its chassis was all too prone to high-speed tankslappers. Add in the poor wet-weather tire and braking performance

typical of the bikes of the time, and the results were frequently disastrous.

The H2, introduced a year later in 1974, was slightly more sane all round. Its motor was less smoky (and 3bhp less powerful); its chassis more stable thanks to less-steep forks and a longer wheelbase. But the H2 was still by far the nastiest, most aggressive and most outrageous bike on the street.

Racing was an obvious progression, and the Kawasaki factory triples, nicknamed 'Green Meanies,' notched plenty of wins in the mid-Seventies, notably in the hands of Mick Grant, Barry Ditchburn and Yvon Duhamel. But tightening emission controls, especially in California, spelled doom for big road-going two-strokes. The H2's reign of motorcycling terror was relatively short.

KAWASAKI 750 H2 (1974)	
Engine	Aircooled two-stroke transverse triple
Capacity	748cc
Claimed power	71bhp at 6800rpm
Weight	205kg (451lbs) dry
Top speed	120mph (192km/h)
Standing quarter-mile	12.5sec/105mph (168km/h)

BMW R90S

The Japanese might have built the most powerful bikes of the early Seventies, and the Italians the most beautiful – but when BMW produced the R90S in 1974 it was regarded by many riders as the best production motorcycle in the world. Here, for the first time ever, was a machine that could offer smooth, comfortable 100mph cruising, plus good handling, excellent reliability and impeccable finish.

The R90S was the latest in a line of flat-twins that stretched all the way back to the Twenties, and its 898cc motor shared the German firm's traditional shaft final drive and pushrod-operated valve layout. Tuned slightly from the base-model R90/6 engine, with increased compression ratio and bigger 38mm Dell'Orto carburetors, the S put out a maximum of 67bhp at 7000rpm.

Straight-line performance was not in the Kawasaki Z1 league, but the Bee-Em had heaps of low-down torque and its top speed of around 125mph was very respectable. More importantly, flat handlebars and a neat bikini fairing allowed the BMW rider to make the most of the twin's relaxed, long-legged power delivery. Handling was up to the job, too, thanks partly to the twin's relatively light weight. Suspension was fairly soft but worked well, despite a certain amount of drive-shaft reaction at the rear. And the pair of front discs gave adequately powerful braking.

BMW's flagship was the ultimate executive express, with a price tag to match. In 1974 it cost considerably more than the Z1 and more than twice as much as Honda's CB750. That money bought a classy smoked paint scheme, a clock on the dashboard, a 200-mile fuel range and a seat comfortable enough to let you use it.

The 90S was not perfect, but by the standards of the day it was pretty damn close. To paraphrase a magazine test at the time, it handled and stopped almost as well as the best Italian sportster; was almost as rapid as the fastest Japanese road-

burner; and was almost as uncomplicated as a good old British twin. When it came to comfort, and the ability to travel at maximum speed with minimum fatigue, the R90S was second to none.

BMW R90S (1974)

Engine	Aircooled 4-valve horizontally-opposed pushrod twin
Capacity	898cc
Claimed power	67bhp at 7000rpm
Weight	215kg (474lbs) wet
Top speed	125mph (200km/h)
Standing quarter-mile	13.2sec/105mph (168km/h)

Above: A set of panniers was the natural addition to BMW's refined executive express, which justified its high price with peerless all-round performance.

Left: The R90S's cockpit fairing and distinctive paintwork made the Bavarian boxer one of the most handsome bikes on the road, as well as one of the best.

Far left: Kawasaki's H2 was the definitive high-performance two-stroke of the mid-Seventies: lean, loud, smelly, thirsty and above all outrageously fast.

BENELLI 750 SEI

Benelli's 750 Sei was the bike that seemed to have it all. Backing up its unique attraction of six cylinders with sharp styling and the Italian manufacturer's world pedigree, the Sei boasted a specification as impressive as its shiny mufflers.

The Sei was an interesting mass of contradictions. Its 748cc engine was the world's first modern road-going six, but it contained little advanced engineering and produced a fairly modest 71 bhp. A common criticism was that the SOHC lump was simply one-and-a-half Honda CB500-four motors, though that was not totally fair. The Italian factory had plenty of engineering pedigree of their own, having won a 250cc world road-race title as recently as 1969.

For a six, the engine was commendably narrow, measuring just an inch wider across the crankcases than Honda's CB750. The trio of dual-manifold Dell'Orto carbs left the rider plenty of knee-room, as well as providing crisp throttle response and plenty of smooth midrange torque. But its top speed was another matter. With a large frontal area, the softly-tuned Benelli could barely wheeze past 115mph.

The Sei's chassis showed the Japanese just what could be done with an in-line multi, for despite its big motor the Benelli was remarkably nimble. The frame was a stronger-than-average steel cradle, and held high-quality Italian

Below and left: The Benelli 750 Sei shows off its elegant lines.

cycle-parts. The Marzocchi suspension was typically firm and well-damped, the Pirelli tires gripped well and the twin Brembo front discs gave powerful braking.

Benelli had hoped that the exotic engine layout would make the six hugely popular. But, despite all the flash and the fact that it was actually a very good bike, the Sei never sold well. Other, more down-to-earth figures – particularly its high price and performance – proved more relevant.

Nevertheless, the Sei stayed in production virtually unchanged until the end of the decade. The motor was then enlarged to produce the 900 Sei, which had an extra 6bhp and a neat headlamp fairing but only twin mufflers. The 900, too, was handsome but it was also more expensive.

BENELLI 750 SEI (1975)

Engine	Aircooled 12-valve SOHC transverse six
Capacity	748cc
Claimed power	71bhp at 8900rpm
Weight	220kg (485lbs) dry
Top speed	118mph (189km/h)
Standing quarter-mile	14sec/95mph (152km/h)

MV AGUSTA 750S AMERICA

Fast, loud and expensive, MV's mighty four was the original race-replica: a road-going version of the legendary 'Gallarate fire-engines' that won every 500cc world championship from 1958 to 1974. The MV's price and rarity meant few motorcyclists could ever hope to buy one – but the few who did knew they owned the closest bike yet to a genuine motorcycle grand prix winner.

Such was the MV marque's mystique that road riders had been dreaming about a replica for years, but when the Italian factory first produced a four-cylinder roadster, in 1967, it was a slow and ugly 600cc tourer. The 750S, released four years later, was faster, prettier and MV's first sporting four. It was

the America, launched in 1975, however, that brought the full Agusta glory to the street. Built specially for the US market at the request of the importers (hence the name), it was tuned and styled to resemble the machine on which Phil Read had just won MV's 37th and final world title. Dramatic lines were enhanced by factory-style red-and-silver paintwork, a suede seat and, if required, a full fairing.

At the center sat MV's jewel of an engine, its sandcast cases and gear-driven camshafts providing an unmistakable appearance to match the stirring sound from the shiny straight-through pipes (black mufflers offered a quieter alternative). The aircooled, 790cc four was lumpy at low

speeds but superbly smooth and responsive when revving hard. Its conservative output of 75bhp sent the MV roaring to over 130mph.

The America's chassis was no match for its engine, despite top-notch cycle-parts including Ceriani forks and Scarab disc brakes. Steering was heavy, and in fast bends the bike's weight combined with a weak frame and the extra mass of the shaft-drive system to produce some nasty wobbles. But for all its faults, the MV was a memorable bike to ride.

Both the America and its successor, the 837cc, 85bhp Monza, were flops for financially stricken MV. The intricate motors were costly to produce, and sales never matched expectations. By the end of the decade, the Gallarate firm had abandoned bikes to concentrate its resources on helicopter manufacturing, and a great chapter in motorcycling history had finally ended.

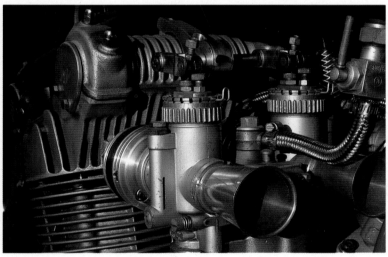

The America (left) was based on MV's earlier 750S four (top), and closely resembled the famous 'Gallarate fire engines'. Its potent twin-cam engine breathed through unfiltered Dell'Orto carburetors (above).

MV AGUSTA 750S AMERICA (1975)

Engine	Aircooled 8-valve DOHC transverse four
Capacity	790cc
Claimed power	75bhp at 8500rpm
Weight	255kg (562lbs) wet
Top speed	133mph (213km/h)
Standing quarter-mile	13sec/105mph (168km/h)

DUCATI 900SS

Not so much a race-replica as a genuine racer with lights and a speedometer, Ducati's 900SS was rolling proof of the beauty that could result from a motorcycle designed purely for speed. Singleminded to the point of being starkly functional, the booming V-twin blended track heritage with a complete absence of frills to provide a uniquely intoxicating ride.

The 900SS was launched in 1975 as a development of the 750SS, which had been produced to cash in on Paul Smart's victory in the prestigious 1972 Imola 200 race. The Bologna factory had intended to make a small number of street-legal bikes closely modeled on Smart's 750 V-twin, but the 750SS was so successful that they built more, then bored out the engine to 864cc to produce the 900SS.

Fabio Taglioni's 90-degree V-twin had already become the Ducati trademark, with cylinders set along the line of the bike, bevel-gear drive to the overhead cams, and desmodromic valve operation (valves closed by cams, instead of springs). Sucking in through huge, unfiltered 40mm Dell'Orto carbs and exhaling freely through Conti pipes, the 900 thundered out torque all the way to 8000rpm.

Maximum power was a healthy 79bhp, and the Ducati's lack of size and weight was a big help to performance. Cut lean, and lacking even the luxury of indicators or an electric starter, the 900SS scaled a competitive 414lbs. With its rider gripping clip-ons behind the silver-and-blue half-fairing, the SS would rumble to over 130mph.

Equally importantly, the solid handling provided by its rigid steel frame and stiff Marzocchi suspension meant that the 900 could be held flat out through bends that forced rivals to shut off. And when the rider did need to slow, there were no better brakes in motorcycling than the Ducati's trio of Brembo discs.

The 900SS remained in production for almost a decade, although many later models lost their edge with the fitment of filtered 32mm carbs and restrictive Lafranconi mufflers. The black-and-gold SS introduced in 1978 retained the original's uncompromising nature, though. And that year Mike Hailwood rode a Ducati to an emotional TT victory, which led to a successful Mike Hailwood Replica 900SS, with a full fairing in Hailwood's green-and-red colors.

Left: The 900SS's purposeful appearance was backed-up by effortless performance from the V-twin engine (inset).

DUCATI 900SS (1975)	
Engine	Aircooled 4-valve SOHC desmodromic 90-degree V-twin
Capacity	864cc
Claimed power	79bhp at 7000rpm
Weight	188kg (414lbs) dry
Top speed	132mph (211km/h)
Standing quarter-mile	13sec/100mph (160km/h)

LAVERDA JOTA 1000

Motorbikes did not come any more muscular than the Jota which, with its rugged styling, magnificent three-cylinder engine and wailing exhaust note, was *the* definitive superbike of the late Seventies. Built by a small family firm that also produced agricultural machinery, the Jota was big, brutal and blindingly fast; the ultimate in hairy-chested Italian motorcycling machismo.

This most famous of all Laverda's 981cc aircooled triples resulted from a collaboration between the Breganze firm and their British importer. At the importer's request, Laverda fitted their existing 3C triple with the hot cams and high-compression pistons used by factory endurance racers. Free-breathing pipes completed a snarling 90bhp beast that stormed to a top speed of close to 140mph.

The Laverda was a tall, heavy bike that required a firm hand to make it change direction, and was prone to occa-

sional high-speed instability. But for the most part it handled well, with the help of typically firm Ceriani suspension. Roadholding was excellent; the braking power from three big Brembo discs immense. The Jota was the world's fastest production roadster in 1976, and went on to prove its superiority with numerous production-race victories.

The triple was a uniquely demanding bike to ride, its thrilling acceleration combining with the unfaired riding position, numbing engine vibration and a wrist-punishingly heavy clutch to make every journey an event. In other respects the Laverda was well-equipped, as befitted its premium price, with finish and electrics that were excellent.

In 1978 Laverda enlarged the motor to produce a 1200 that had more midrange, although no more peak power. In 1980 they gave the Jota a half-fairing, and in 1982 smoothed the three-cylinder engine by redesigning it with equal, 120-degree firing intervals, in place of the original 180-degree (two pistons up, one down) arrangement.

But the wild days were coming to a close, and a year later Laverda introduced the RGS1000, with softer cams, rounded bodywork, a lower frame and heavily-silenced exhaust. The RGS, and the tuned Corsa and SFC1000 models that followed it, were fast, fine motorcycles. But they lacked the raw, animal appeal that had made the Jota so special.

LAVERDA JOTA 1000 (1976)

Engine	Aircooled 6-valve DOHC transverse triple
Capacity	981cc
Claimed power	90bhp at 8000rpm
Weight	236kg (520lbs) wet
Top speed	138mph (221km/h)
Standing quarter-mile	12.5sec/110mph (176km/h)

Left: The Jota's muscular, no-nonsense look survived the Seventies almost unchanged. Humped seat and rearset footrests show this is one of the last 180-degree models.

Above: No motorcycle on the roads could match the big Laverda in its heyday, thanks primarily to the thunderous power of its twin-cam, 90bhp three-cylinder engine.

MOTO GUZZI 850 LE MANS (1976)

Engine	Aircooled 4-valve pushrod 90-degree transverse V-twin
Capacity	844cc
Claimed power	80bhp at 7300rpm
Weight	216kg (476lbs) wet
Top speed	132mph (211km/h)
Standing quarter-mile	13.5sec/105mph (168km/h)

Above: Guzzi's trademark 90-degree V-twin engine, with cylinders placed across the line of the bike, gave the Le Mans thunderous midrange torque and easy high-speed cruising.

Right: The handsome Mk 1 Le Mans was dominated visually by its tiny flyscreen and big aircooled cylinders. The fully-faired Mk 2 was more comfortable at speed, but lacked charisma.

MOTO GUZZI 850 LE MANS

Of all the great Italian bikes of the late Seventies, Moto Guzzi's 850 Le Mans was perhaps the most magical of all. Around the unlikeliest of powerplants – a 90-degree V-twin based on a motor designed for a wartime armored-car – Guzzi constructed a sportster that combined thrilling speed with excellent handling and looks that were nothing short of absolutely stunning.

The firm from the banks of Lake Como had been building

bikes since the Twenties, earning a fine reputation and collecting eight world road-race titles along the way. They produced the Le Mans in 1976 by enlarging and tuning the transverse-mounted engine of their existing 750 S3 roadster – itself a rapid and handsome machine – and adding a handlebar fairing, curvaceous petrol tank, strikingly angular seat and paintwork in Italian racing red.

The aircooled 844cc lump was a fairly crude device with

pushrod valve operation and a notchy five-speed gearbox. But fitted with high-compression pistons, and breathing through a brace of unfiltered 36mm Dell'Orto carburetors, the Le Mans kicked-out 80bhp and delivered 130mph-plus performance with punchy midrange acceleration and a smooth, long-legged feel.

A strong steel frame and state-of-the-art suspension gave good, stable handling despite the occasionally unsettling effect of the shaft final drive. Braking was powerful and reliable, thanks to three big Brembo discs linked by Guzzi's unique system. The handlebar lever operated one front disc; the foot pedal the other plus the rear.

The Le Mans was less hard edged than its rivals from Laverda and Ducati, delivering serious speed with a relaxed quality that made it arguably the ultimate high-speed road-burner. But the factory could not produce a worthy successor. The Mk2 version of 1979 was slower, though it at least gave its rider the benefit of an angular full fairing. The 1982-model Mk 3 regained some power.

Guzzi's increasingly desperate development reached a nadir three years later with the 949cc Mk 4, which suffered from clumsy styling and a 16-inch front wheel that did nothing to improve handling. It was all a far cry from the elegance of the original 850 Le Mans.

HARLEY-DAVIDSON XLCR1000

There have been few more unlikely superbikes than Harley-Davidson's XLCR Cafe Racer, the big black V-twin released in 1977. Many years earlier, the Milwaukee firm had built some of the fastest bikes in the world. But as the sole model with sporting pretensions in Harley's long list of cruisers and tourers, the Cafe Racer stood very much alone.

The newcomer was based on Harley's famous Sportster, which had been a high-performance model itself when released in 1952 but had long since abandoned ideas about living up to its name. Holding the familiar 45-degree motor in a slightly re-engineered and heavily restyled rolling chassis, the Cafe Racer was intended to attract a new breed of motorcycling customer.

On looks alone, it would have succeeded. Reputedly conceived and styled by Harley design director Willie G Davidson himself, the Cafe Racer was long, lean and dressed elegantly in black from top to toe. Its engine was stock Sportster, which meant a 998cc lump with pushrod valve operation, four-speed gearbox and a claimed peak output of 61bhp at 6200rpm.

The V-twin motor was mounted solidly in a hybrid frame consisting of a Sportster front-end plus parts from Harley's XR750 racebike. Forks and shocks were borrowed from the Sportster, though the Cafe Racer was at least treated to a second front disc brake and Goodyear tires.

The Cafe Racer's basic problem was that although Harley's age-old engine and chassis technology was okay for a laid-back cruiser, it just didn't work for a bike with flat bars, rearset footpegs and thoughts of serious speed. The big V-twin kicked-out lots of low-down torque, and would send the 'Hawg' thundering up to 120mph.

Ever-present vibration made such speeds impossible for long, though, and even much slower use resulted in a numb rider and in bits of the bike coming loose. Crude suspension and lack of ground clearance made fast cornering hairy, especially on bumpy roads.

At the time the XLCR did not appeal either to sporting riders or to the traditional Harley bunch, but history has treated it kindly. In retrospect, the Cafe Racer's looks, noise and charisma more than make up for its lack of performance.

HARLEY-DAVIDSON XLCR1000 (1977)

Engine	Aircooled 4-valve 45-degree pushrod V-twin
Capacity	998cc
Claimed power	61bhp at 6200rpm
Weight	234kg (515lbs) wet
Top speed	120mph (192km/h)
Standing quarter-mile	14sec/95mph (152km/h)

Right: The fine lines of the Harley-Davidson XLCR1000 were reputedly conceived and styled by the company's design director, Willie G Davidson.

SUZUKI GS1000

To appreciate the impact of Suzuki's GS1000 it's necessary to put yourself in the place of a speed-hungry motorcyclist at the beginning of 1978. Back then, the Japanese produced several powerful, sophisticated bikes, from Honda's CB750 and Gold Wing to Kawasaki's Z1000. But if you wanted a machine that really *handled*, it had to be European, preferably from Guzzi, Ducati, Laverda or even BMW.

The GS1000 changed all that at a stroke. Combining a typical four-cylinder engine with a chassis whose layout was equally conventional, it heralded a second generation of Japanese superbike design. Not only was the GS faster than anything that had come out of the East before, but more importantly its stability and cornering ability allowed that engine performance to be used to the full.

For such a star, the GS had an unspectacular appearance, with restrained styling, slightly raised bars and an aircooled, 997cc twin-cam engine that resembled those of Suzuki's own GS750 – launched a year earlier – and Kawasaki's Z1000. But what an engine! Not only did the newcomer make 4bhp more power than the benchmark Kawa, with a peak of 87bhp. It also developed more torque throughout the range, and was lighter and equally reliable.

A strong, twin-downtube frame held suspension more sophisticated than anything previously seen on a mass-produced roadster. Front forks were air-assisted, and the shocks could be adjusted for rebound damping as well as for the normal preload. Powerful triple disc brakes were marred only by a slight wet-weather delay typical of the time.

It added-up to a stunning new superbike, as happy scorching smoothly to its 135mph top speed as it was cruising effortlessly on the freeway or being hustled along a twisty country road. Kawasaki's Z1000, for so long the 'King,' was deposed by a bike that was superior in virtually every respect.

In 1980 Suzuki produced the GS1000S by adding a neat top-half fairing. The GS1000G tourer that arrived a year later was less successful, its shaft-drive and soft suspension ruining the handling, and by then the basic model had been replaced by the 16-valve GSX1100. But the original GS1000 will long be remembered as the bike with which the Japanese finally got everything right.

SUZUKI GS1000 (1978)

Engine	Aircooled 8-valve DOHC transverse four
Capacity	997cc
Claimed power	87bhp at 8000rpm
Weight	242kg (533lbs) wet
Top speed	135mph (216km/h)
Standing quarter-mile	12sec/108mph (173km/h)

Left: Styling of the original GS1000 was pleasant but unspectacular – a phrase that certainly could not be used to describe the four-cylinder Suzuki's shattering performance.

Inset: The GS's aircooled, twin-cam engine was similar in layout to that of Kawasaki's Z1000, but the 87bhp Suzuki outperformed its previously dominant rival in most respects.

YAMAHA XS1100

The attraction of Yamaha's XS1100 was basic and unforgettable. At about 50mph in top gear, the rider simply cracked open the throttle – and then held on tight as the Yam responded instantly with arm-wrenching acceleration the like of which had not been known before. With 1101cc of capacity giving a peak output of 95bhp and massive low-rev urge, the big black four-cylinder XS motor was one altogether mighty powerplant.

Unfortunately, the Yamaha's weight – some 600lbs with a full tank of fuel – was an equally relevant statistic. The XS, launched in 1978, was a Japanese superbike of the old school: a big, powerful engine in a big, heavy chassis. Not so much XS as excess. Its arrival coincided with that of Suzuki's 65lbs lighter and much more nimble GS1000. After riding both bikes, the Yam's straight-line stomp seemed of somewhat limited appeal.

This was still some engine, though. Technically unremarkable, with twin cams opening two valves per cylinder, it followed Yamaha's earlier XS750 triple in using shaft final drive. The 1100 motor was tuned for maximum midrange response, producing usable torque as low as 2000 rpm and a class-leading peak of 66.5ft.lb at 6500rpm.

Yamaha's engineers had obviously been worried about chassis strength, because the XS's steel duplex-cradle frame was heavily braced. This added to the weight and, although suspension was reasonable, the Yam could not hide its bulk on the road. In slow bends it felt ponderous; at higher speed, stability was marginal in anything other than a straight line.

The XS1100 was at least fairly comfortable, despite its high handlebars, thanks mainly to the engine's smoothness and the generous seat. With useful touches such as self-canceling indicators, a big tank and a fuel gauge, it was well equipped, too. The XS was at its best as a gentle tourer, loaded with luggage and fitted with a big fairing.

Yamaha apparently did not think so, though, and in 1981 introduced the XS1100 Sport, complete with handlebar fairing, smaller petrol tank and black paintwork. The Sport was a potent and mean-looking machine, with similar visual appeal to Harley's Cafe Racer. Unfortunately, for sports riding it was equally out of its depth.

Above: The shaft-drive engine was for its supply of low-speed torque.

Right: The Yamaha couldn't disguise its size even in front of a mountain.

YAMAHA XS1100 (1978)

Engine	Aircooled 8-valve DOHC transverse four
Capacity	1101cc
Claimed power	95bhp at 8000rpm
Weight	271kg (598lbs) wet
Top speed	135mph (216km/h)
Standing quarter-mile	12.3sec/110mph (176km/h)

HONDA CBX1000

Unique in its performance, its looks, its engineering and its spine-tingling exhaust sound, the six-cylinder CBX1000 was both a striking corporate statement and a magnificent sports bike. Introduced in 1978 to boost a tired Honda range, the CBX was in a class of its own among Japanese bikes for sheer glamor and singleminded sporting intent.

Its aircooled, DOHC, 24-valve motor was inspired by Honda's hugely successful racing multis of the Sixties. (The roadster's chief designer, Shoichiro Irimajiri, had been responsible for several of the racebikes too.) With its angled-forward cylinders fed by a bank of six carburetors, the 1047cc unit produced a maximum of 105bhp at 9000rpm. Its alternator's position on a secondary shaft above the gearbox meant the six was barely wider than most fours.

Designed from the outset as a no-compromise sportster, the CBX used its engine as a stressed member of a tubular frame. Neat, understated bodywork and the frame's lack of downtubes emphasized the bare-chested bravado of the shiny six-pot powerplant. Using twin mufflers kept down weight, as did the alloy fork yokes, plastic mudguards and even magnesium engine covers.

Performance was shattering, combining ease of use with the hardest acceleration yet produced by a streetbike. At low revs, the six was docile and supremely smooth, responding crisply without great urgency below about 6000rpm. Above that figure the CBX came alive, leaping toward its 135mph top speed with unmatched ferocity and a memorable, high-pitched whistle from its exhaust.

Despite Honda's efforts the CBX was no lightweight, scaling 572lbs with of gallon a gas. But its frame was stiff, suspension pretty good, and ground clearance generous. The Honda was easy to steer, it was stable (at least provided its tires were not too worn), and its triple disc brakes gave plenty of power and feel.

Sadly for Honda, the CBX1000's brilliance was not matched by sales success, especially in the American market. In 1981 the bike was softened with a big fairing, slightly detuned engine and air-assisted suspension. The CBX1000-B was a competent bike, and it sold quite well in the States. But it had neither the performance nor the raw appeal of the original, sensational Six.

HONDA CBX1000 (1978)

Engine	Aircooled 24-valve DOHC transverse six
Capacity	1047cc
Claimed power	105bhp at 9000rpm
Weight	260kg (572lbs) wet
Top speed	135mph (216km/h)
Standing quarter-mile	12sec/115mph (184km/h)

Left: The original CBX was a singleminded sports bike, its looks and personality dominated totally by that magnificent six-cylinder powerplant.

Right: The softer, fully-faired CBX-B sold quite well in America, but it had neither the performance nor the purity of design that had made Honda's first Six so special.

HARRIS MAGNUM

Despite the collapse of the British motorcycle industry, some of the fastest and finest bikes on the roads in the late Seventies were created in the country once famous for Broughs and BSAs. Based on Japanese four-cylinder engines, usually from Kawasaki or Honda, these were the specials: race-developed machines built by small firms such as Rickman, Dresda and Peckett & McNab.

Most famous and popular was the Magnum, the single-seat special constructed by Hertford-based brothers Steve and Lester Harris. Closely based on the firm's successful Formula One and endurance racers, the Magnum provided a package of sleek styling, light weight and fine handling that surpassed anything from the major manufacturers.

The key to the Magnum was its chassis, most importantly the frame of Reynolds 531 steel tubing. Almost identical to frames built for bikes competing in races such as the Bol d'Or 24 hours, the hand-welded Magnum trellis brought new levels of rigidity to the street. Rear suspension comprised a cantilever swing-arm with single De Carbon shock absorber. Front fork choice was left to the customer, who usually specified top-quality aftermarket items from Marzocchi or Betor. Likewise the brakes and wheels, which were generally racing components from specialists such as Lockheed and Dymag.

The engine was often tuned with racing carbs and a free-breathing Harris four-into-one exhaust. Many owners went further, with racing camshafts, big-bore kits and high-compression pistons that took a Kawasaki Z1000's output to 125bhp or more.

Adding low clip-on bars, a thinly padded single seat and a twin-headlamp fairing completed a fearsome machine that brought a new dimension to road-going motorcycling. A well set up Magnum was good for 140mph, with handling and braking to match. The aggressive riding position made that performance usable, too, though at the expense of comfort at slower speeds.

Limitless choice of engine tune and cycle-parts meant no two Magnums were identical. But early models can be divided into two versions: the angular original and the smoother Mk II styled by Jan Fellstrom (famous for work on Suzuki's Katana). The look was different, but the Harris Magnum sensation remained the same: speed, noise and racetrack handling, from the definitive British special.

HARRIS MAGNUM I (1979)

Engine	Aircooled 8-valve DOHC transverse four (Kawasaki)
Capacity	1015cc
Claimed power	110bhp at 8500rpm
Weight	218kg (480lbs) wet
Top speed	140mph (224km/h)
Standing quarter-mile	11.7sec/120mph (192km/h)

Above: Many Magnum builders opted for a highly-tuned Kawasaki motor.

MOTO MARTIN

Endurance racing is a particularly French event, so it's natural that over the years many cafe-racers should be built there, inspired by the machines raced at the Le Mans and Bol d'Or 24 hours. France's best-known brand in the late Seventies and early Eighties was Moto Martin, the Brittany-based firm that built endurance-style specials based on engines as varied as Suzuki's GT750 triple, Kawasaki's Z1000 four and even Honda's CBX1000 six.

Georges Martin's early frames were based on a tubular spine running horizontally above the motor, but the later designs for which he became known used thinner chrome-molybdenum tubes that encircled the engine. Like many special builders at the time, he used a cantilever swing-arm with De Carbon monoshock. Forks and wheels were to Martin's own specification, generally fitted with Brembo brakes and Michelin tires.

Much of Moto Martin's appeal was based on futuristic, curvaceous styling, often finished with a factory race-team paint scheme accurate to the smallest sponsor's sticker. The classic design featured a twin-headlamp fairing, plus a fiberglass tank-seat unit with no room for a passenger. Handlebars were low; footrests high. Between the bulging frame tubes was a highly-tuned Kawasaki Z1000 lump.

Speed was never in question with a Martin, and a genuine 140mph was well within the capability of a Kawasaki-engined special. The racy riding position and efficient fairing made that performance temptingly usable, too. And no matter what the speed, the Martin rider could always rely on the rigid chassis for complete stability.

The French machines had less genuine racetrack development than rivals from firms such as Harris, though. That sometimes showed when their long wheelbase and conservative, road-biased steering geometry made the rider work hard through a series of bends. Martins required commitment – but ridden forcefully these bikes were among the very quickest on the roads.

Martin went on to produce bikes based on Suzuki's 16-valve GSX1100 and Honda's CB900, but perhaps best of all was the Martin CBX1000 introduced in early 1980. Combining Honda's huge six-cylinder motor with a Martin frame, swoopy half-fairing and tuneful exhaust system produced a bike that was unbeatable for outrageous cafe-racer style.

MOTO MARTIN CBX1000(1980)

Engine	Aircooled 24-valve DOHC transverse six (Honda)
Capacity	1047cc
Claimed power	110bhp at 9000rpm
Weight	240kg (528lbs) wet
Top speed	140mph (224km/h)
Standing quarter-mile	11.7sec/120mph (192km/h)

Above: The Honda CBX1000-engined model was the most stylish Martin of all.

KAWASAKI Z1300

Kawasaki's gargantuan Z1300 epitomized the two-wheeled excess of the late Seventies. With six watercooled cylinders, an output of 120bhp and a fueled-up weight of over 700lbs, the Z13 was the most outrageous product yet of a period in which superbikes had become ever bigger, heavier and more complex.

Even as the Kawasaki was being launched, the then West German government was implementing a 100bhp limit amid mutterings that the two events were connected. But for most motorcyclists, the Z1300's most controversial feature was not the power of its engine but the sheer bulk of the slab-sided monster built to carry it.

The Z13 weighed 100lbs more than Honda's CBX1000, and ironically the Kawasaki's large radiator obscured its engine to leave the 'Zed' with little of the visual impact of Honda's Six. The 1286cc, twin-cam powerplant had unusually long-stroke dimensions of 62 × 71mm (the CBX, more typically, measured 64.5 × 53.4mm). This kept width down but resulted in a tall motor whose weight was increased further by shaft final drive.

A massive steel frame and well-chosen suspension at least meant the Z1300's handling was surprisingly good. Just as well, too, for the big bike was quick – dispatching the standing quarter-mile in just 12 seconds. It whistled up to its 135mph top speed without a wobble, was reassuringly stable even in fast curves, and was fitted with both efficient brakes and tires.

But, despite that, the Z1300 wasn't much fun to ride. The Kawa felt as though it would cruise at 100mph for ever, but its

Above: Despite the Z1300's massive size and weight, stunt star Arto Nyqvist makes it fly (right).

high bars and forward-set footpegs meant the rider couldn't keep that up for long. The twin-barrel carburetors and heavily damped transmission conspired to give snatchy throttle response. Although the Six was smooth, it had a busy feel that did not make for particularly relaxed cruising.

The mighty Kawasaki was not a bad motorcycle – but nor was it an outstandingly good one. For all its size, the Z1300 was visually, technically and dynamically unremarkable; simply no faster, more practical or more exciting to ride than several lighter and cheaper alternatives. Its claim to motorcycling fame is that it marked the end of the spiral of increasing size and weight.

KAWASAKI Z1300 (1979)

Engine	Watercooled DOHC 12-valve transverse six
Capacity	1286cc
Claimed power	120bhp at 8000rpm
Weight	305kg (670lbs) wet
Top speed	135mph (216km/h)
Standing quarter-mile	12sec/115mph (184km/h)

HONDA CB1100R

Built in limited numbers with little regard for cost, the super-lative CB1100R was proof of what Honda's engineers could do when they set out to produce the fastest motorcycle in the world. The 1100R was developed from the CB900F four, with the aim of winning production races such as the prestigious Castrol Six-hour in Australia. For the few road riders who could afford it, the R proved as brilliant on the street as it was on the track.

Its motor was based on the CB900's aircooled, 16-valve motor, bored-out to 1062cc and running a higher compression ratio. Peak power was increased by 21 percent to 115bhp, an unprecedented figure for a production sportster. Numerous strengthening modifications throughout the engine included replacement of the connecting rods that had been a weakness of the 900.

The chassis was also based on the 900's, with a streng-

thened steel-tube frame holding similar air-assisted forks. The R's twin shock absorbers were new and sophisticated, featuring remote reservoirs to combat the common problem of overheating damping fluid. The front brake set up was also innovative, with twin-piston calipers biting on the big double discs.

Topped with a streamlined half-fairing and single seat, the 1100R was in a class of its own in 1981. It combined a 145mph top speed with effortless cruising, excellent handling, powerful braking and plenty of ground clearance. It was also smooth, docile, tractable and reliable; as happy crawling in traffic as it was scorching round a racetrack.

The small numbers that were built were snapped-up despite their high price (well over 50 percent more than the CB900F), and the 1100 soon made its mark as a racer. The R won all over the world, often so convincingly – as in the British Streetbike series – that no other model had a chance against it.

Honda made some changes even so, fitting a full fairing in 1982 to cure a slight high-speed weave. That year's model, the 1100R-B, also had a pillion seat, new forks and wider wheels; the R-C of 1983 gained metallic paint and a box-section alloy swing-arm. One thing that didn't change was the 1100R's position at the head of the pack.

Left: Looks, power, handling and comfort made the CB1100 an unbeatable roadster. Young Australian ace Wayne Gardner (inset) rode the Honda to numerous wins.

Above: Single seat and superior remote-reservoir shocks emphasized the Honda's no-compromise approach to high performance.

HONDA CB1100R (1981)

Engine	Aircooled 16-valve DOHC transverse four
Capacity	1062cc
Claimed power	115bhp at 9000rpm
Weight	235kg (518lbs) dry
Top speed	145mph (232km/h)
Standing quarter-mile	11.5sec/118mph (185km/h)

HONDA CX500 TURBO

Turbocharging was a two-wheeled phenomenon that became all the rage in the early Eighties, before being blown away when the motorcycling public – and eventually the manufacturers – realized that talk of easy extra performance was merely hot air. No bike summed up the folly of forced induction better than the first of the breed: Honda's CX500 Turbo.

The very idea of the CX Turbo was perverse. Turbocharging is best suited to large, multi-cylinder engines producing small, regular power impulses. The CX engine, a 497cc watercooled 80-degree V-twin, was virtually the least suitable powerplant Honda could have chosen – which suggested the Turbo was intended more as a statement of corporate prowess than as a sensible motorcycle.

The humble CX motor, with its pushrod valve operation and shaft final drive, required the world's smallest turbocharger. Built by specialists IHI to Honda's spec, its blades measured less than two inches in diameter and spun at 200,000rpm to raise the CX's output from 50 to 82bhp at 8000rpm. Needless to say, many engine components were uprated to cope.

Honda's work did not stop with the motor, for the Turbo was intended as a rolling showcase for technology including a digital ignition and fuel-injection system, TRAC anti-dive, twin-piston brake calipers, and Pro-Link single-shock rear suspension. Most striking of all was the enormous pearl-white fairing, complete with integral indicators and comprehensive instruments.

The fairing was superb, allowing high-speed cruising in unprecedented comfort, and the CX handled remarkably well considering its fueled-up weight of almost 600lbs. But the Honda wasn't particularly fast, with sluggish acceleration and a top speed of 125mph. And it suffered from turbo-lag, the delay between throttle opening and engine response.

As a grand-tourer the Turbo was impressive, but it could not overcome the inevitable penalties of complexity, weight and expense. A year later Honda uprated it by producing the CX650 Turbo, complete with more power, less lag, storming acceleration and a top speed of 135mph.

But for all its new-found flair, the Turbo was still no quicker than many simpler and cheaper alternatives. Each of the 'Big Four' Japanese manufacturers had a try before admitting defeat, and finally the turbocharging revolution came to an end.

HONDA CX500 TURBO (1982)

Engine	Watercooled 6-valve pushrod 80-degree transverse V-twin, turbocharged
Capacity	497cc
Claimed power	82bhp at 8000rpm
Weight	240kg (527lbs) dry
Top speed	125mph (200km/h)
Standing quarter-mile	12.5sec/100mph (160km/h)

Left: Dramatically shaped fairing helped make the Turbo a comfortable bike.

Inset: A middleweight V-twin was not suitable for a turbocharger.

SUZUKI GSX1100S KATANA

When launched in 1982 it was stunning – a raw, aggressively styled sportster the like of which had never been seen before from Japan. And over 10 years later it's *still* visually striking – regarded by many enthusiasts as a classic example of two-wheeled design, and commemorated by Suzuki with their recent 250 and 400cc replicas.

The GSX1100S Katana, with its radical looks, four-cylinder engine and uncompromising high-performance approach, paved the way for the modern Japanese race-replica. For a mass-produced machine its hard-edged nature was a revelation in a period dominated by the upright riding position of the 'Universal Japanese Motorcycle.'

The Katana was based on Suzuki's outstanding GSX1100, which had replaced the GS1000 two years earlier. Its bold styling involved an integrated package of nose fairing, clocks, humped tank and combined seat and sidepanel assembly. 'Katana' was a Japanese word for a Samurai warrior's ceremonial sword, and suited Suzuki's latter day sharp silver blade perfectly.

Tuning the GSX1100's aircooled, 16-valve motor (by de-restricting the airbox, modifying carburetors and valve timing, and lightening the alternator) gave a maximum of 111bhp at 8500rpm. The standard bike's steel twin-cradle frame was basically unchanged, but new yokes gave a little extra rake for increased stability. Forks were fitted with

hydraulic anti-dive, Suzuki's latest grand-prix developed extra; the twin shocks received stiffer springs.

Straight-line performance was similar to the GSX's, with a top speed of over 140mph and strong, smooth midrange acceleration. At high speeds the Katana had the edge. Its clip-ons and rearset footpegs combined with the tiny flyscreen to improve aerodynamics and wind protection. The frame and firm suspension were well up to hard cornering, and the triple disc brakes were powerful. Only its hard Japanese tires let the Suzuki down.

Naturally, there were compromises. The racy riding position was impractical in town, and the narrow clip-ons and conservative geometry made for heavy steering. The seat was uncomfortable, especially for a pillion, and at almost 550lbs the 'Kat' was no lightweight. The Suzuki's looks and speed combined with a reasonable price to ensure it was a big success. The Katana bridged the gap between harsh Italian sportsters and bland UJMs, proving that the Japanese too could provide performance with originality and style.

Above: Katana's styling was outrageous in 1982.

Above left: Firm suspension and a strong

frame gave good handling.

Below left: Some riders added a tuned motor and aftermarket exhaust system.

SUZUKI GSX1100S KATANA (1982)

Engine	Aircooled 16-valve DOHC transverse four
Capacity	1075cc
Claimed power	111bhp at 8500rpm
Weight	248kg (545lbs) wet
Top speed	143mph (229km/h)
Standing quarter-mile	11.6sec/117mph (187km/h)

43

KAWASAKI GPZ900R

No sports bike made a more lasting impact on the Eighties than the GPZ900R. Kawasaki's first watercooled four stormed on to the scene in 1984, becoming an instant hit with its blend of power, compact size and sharp handling. The Ninja, as the 900R was known officially in most countries, was still selling, barely modified, well into the Nineties.

Kawasaki's earlier aircooled fours, all with two valves per cylinder, had established a formidable reputation but the Ninja's 908cc watercooled lump proved a worthy successor. It featured a 16-valve cylinder head plus developments including a balancer shaft, camchain at the end of the crank, and alternator above the six-speed gearbox. It was small, light and powerful, though its 113bhp peak was slightly below that of the old GPz1100.

The rest of the GPZ continued the theme of high performance with minimum size and weight. Its frame used the engine as a stressed member, combining steel main tubes with an alloy rear subframe. Forks were 38mm units with anti-dive; rear suspension Kawasaki's Uni-Trak monoshock with air-assistance and adjustable rebound damping.

The sharply styled full fairing did a fair job of shielding the rider, who leant forward to flattish bars, with feet on slightly rearset pegs. The Ninja was low and respectably light – and most of all it was fast. Top speed was over 150mph, with dramatic acceleration above 6000rpm and searing speed from 8000rpm to the 10,500rpm redline.

Above: The GPZ's 16-inch front wheel was swapped for a 17-incher.

Above right: The Kawasaki's profile allowed 150mph-plus performance.

Right: Watercooled, 16-valve engine proved a fine successor to Kawasaki's line of aircooled fours.

Equally importantly, it was docile at low speed and supremely controllable. The rigid frame, firm suspension and 16-inch front wheel gave stability with light, precise steering. Brakes were superbly powerful, with the only fault a slight harshness in the forks.

The Kawasaki was also very practical for a sportster, combining a generous fuel range with surprising comfort and neat details such as luggage hooks and a strong grab-rail. It remained unchanged until 1990, when it was updated with thicker forks, wider wheels, better brakes and a 17-inch front wheel. And as its sporting rivals became faster and lighter, the once-mighty Ninja moved gracefully into a new role as a budget-priced sports-tourer.

KAWASAKI GPZ900R (1984)

Engine	Watercooled 16-valve DOHC transverse four
Capacity	908cc
Claimed power	113bhp at 9500rpm
Weight	236kg (520lbs) wet
Top speed	155mph (248km/h)
Standing quarter-mile	11.2sec/120mph (192km/h)

YAMAHA FJ1100

Yamaha's big FJ models have been among the world's best sports-tourers for so long that it's easy to forget that the original FJ1100 forged a reputation as a peerless long-distance roadburner almost by accident. When launched in 1984 it was advertized as an 'out-and-out high performance sports machine,' but was outshone by the simultaneous arrival of Kawasaki's faster GPZ900R. Only then was the softer FJ recast in a *gran turismo* role to which it proved perfectly suited.

The FJ1100's appearance in 1984 was remarkable because Yamaha's previous attempts to produce a superbike had been limited to uncompetitive machines such as the XS1100 and XJ900. The FJ changed all that instantly. In any previous year it would have been outstanding even as a sportster, with its striking, aerodynamic looks, high-profile chassis and powerful 1097cc engine. There was little new technology in the motor, a 16-valve development of Yamaha's long line of aircooled fours. But its performance was breathtaking, not just for the peak output of 125bhp at 9000rpm but also for the way the big lump delivered seamless torque virtually from tickover to redline.

The frame was spectacular, with rectangular-section steel main tubes that ran up from the swing-arm pivot, around the cylinder head and continued around the forks before joining at the front of the bike. It worked superbly well, and the Yamaha combined its 150mph top speed and glorious engine flexibility with rock-solid stability and pleasantly neutral handling.

Suspension was slightly soft for hard riding, conspiring with the 16-inch wheels to reduce ground clearance, but potent brakes helped ensure that few bikes were quicker on the road. The Yamaha's combination of efficient fairing, relaxed riding position, broad seat, generous fuel range and effortless power delivery meant that nothing could match the FJ on a fast long-distance blast.

In subsequent years Yamaha made numerous refinements to keep the FJ competitive. In 1986 its motor was bored out to 1188cc to produce the even torquier FJ1200; two years later saw the introduction of a 17-inch front wheel. In 1991 the Yamaha gained the rubber-mounted engine and anti-lock brakes that made it a more competent all-rounder than ever.

YAMAHA FJ1100 (1984)

Engine	Aircooled 16-valve DOHC transverse four
Capacity	1097cc
Claimed power	125bhp at 9000rpm
Weight	245kg (540lbs) wet
Top speed	150mph (240km/h)
Standing quarter-mile	11.4sec/118mph (189km/h)

YAMAHA FZ750

Following hot on the heels of the FJ1100, the superbly capable FZ750 was further proof that Yamaha – long famous for small-capacity two-strokes – had finally discovered the art of building big four-strokes, too. Outstanding in almost every respect, the FZ broadened the horizons of 750cc performance and marked the arrival of a new generation of Yamaha superbikes.

The FZ's engine was revolutionary: a watercooled, 749cc twin-cam four, containing no fewer than 20 tiny valves and with cylinders angled forward at 45 degrees. Tilting the block moved the center of gravity forward and down. It also allowed the bank of four Mikuni downdraft carburetors, placed where the cylinder head would normally be, a straight run to the engine.

Yamaha claimed their five-valves-per-cylinder layout (three inlets, two exhaust) gave significant breathing improvements over conventional four-valve designs, and the FZ motor's performance was difficult to fault. Maximum power

was a claimed 105bhp at 10,500rpm. More impressive still was the broad spread of power through the range.

The chassis was relatively conservative, based around a frame that followed the FJ1100's in using rectangular-section steel tubes. Air-assisted forks held the 16-inch front wheel that was all the rage in 1985; rear suspension was a vertical monoshock.

Everything came together to produce the best all-round package yet from a 750. The engine was magnificent, allowing smooth, instant acceleration from the lowest speeds – or alternatively revving hard to send the FZ howling to over 140mph. The motor was also smooth, reliable and economical on fuel – and the valves needed adjusting only every 28,000 miles.

Handling was precise yet stable, the chassis let down only by a front brake that lacked the bite of rival systems. The fairly upright riding position allowed comfortable cruising, although the half-fairing's screen was slightly low for sustained high speeds.

Such minor faults should not have prevented the Yam becoming hugely popular, but the plainly styled FZ was overshadowed by Suzuki's more glamorous GSX-R750. Slow initial sales improved slightly a year later when the FZ gained a full fairing. But even later refinements such as a four-into-one exhaust and a 17-inch front wheel did not bring the FZ750 the success it deserved.

YAMAHA FZ750 (1985)	
Engine	Watercooled 20-valve DOHC transverse four
Capacity	749cc
Claimed power	105bhp at 10,500rpm
Weight	209kg (460lbs) dry
Top speed	144mph (230km/h)
Standing quarter-mile	11.5sec/116mph (186km/h)

Above: The original FZ750 combined fine handling with a tractable motor whose 20-valve layout has formed the basis for many watercooled fours.

Right: Adding a full fairing gave the FZ a tidier look, but not the sales success that the bike's all-round excellence merited.

Above left: Designed as a sports bike, the FJ1100 proved hugely successful as a comfortable, high-speed sports-tourer.

SUZUKI GSX-R750

Outrageously fast, light and singleminded, Suzuki's GSX-R750 rewrote the rules of high-performance motorcycling in 1985. This was the original Japanese race-replica: a bold copy of Suzuki's factory endurance machines. It combined a powerful new engine with a chassis designed solely to reduce weight and increase speed. The result was almost invincible.

A few figures illustrate the lengths Suzuki's engineers went to in providing unprecedented 750cc performance. The GSX-R's power output of 100bhp at 10,500rpm was a 10 percent improvement on its GSX750 predecessor. More importantly, the fully faired GSX-R weighed just 388lbs dry – less than most 550s, and 70lbs down on Yamaha's FZ750.

The Suzuki's aluminum frame contained a mixture of cast sections and extruded rails, and weighed under half as much as the GSX's steel trellis. Forks were a hefty 41mm thick, holding a front wheel 18 inches in diameter instead of the normal 16. Suzuki claimed this was to facilitate endurance-race wheel changes; in the GSX-R's case it rang true.

Equal care was taken to reduce weight in the motor, a much-modified version of the aircooled, 16-valve GSX lump. Oilcooling – by passing engine oil through the cylinder head, then a large radiator – was lighter than rival watercooling systems. Most engine components were reduced in size; the cam-cover was lightweight magnesium.

Every aspect of the GSX-R was dedicated to speed: racy twin-headlamp fairing, foam-backed instruments, clip-on bars, rearset pegs, lightweight four-into-one exhaust. The Suzuki lived up to the image. The engine was flat below 7000rpm, then took off in thrilling style toward the 11,000rpm redline and a top speed of 140mph plus.

Every ride became a frenzy of hard acceleration and frantic flicking through the six-speed gearbox. Handling was quite slow but neutral at most speeds, marred by slight high-speed instability that was cured, a year later, by a longer swing-arm. Braking power from big front discs with four-piston calipers was immense.

The GSX-R's design was radical – and it worked. Soon the world's roads and racetracks were swarming with screaming Suzukis, and the cult of the race-replica was established. After the GSX-R750, motorcycling on the limit would never be quite the same again.

SUZUKI GSX-R750 (1985)	
Engine	Oilcooled 16-valve DOHC transverse four
Capacity	749cc
Claimed power	100bhp at 10,500rpm
Weight	176kg (388lbs) dry
Top speed	146mph (234km/h)
Standing quarter-mile	11.5sec/116mph (186km/h)

Left: Built purely for speed, the GSX-R750 backed-up its racy fairing and powerful, oilcooled motor with a remarkably lightweight chassis.

Inset: Suzuki's 750cc factory endurance race bike provided very obvious inspiration for the GSX-R roadster's styling and alloy frame technology.

YAMAHA VMX1200 V-MAX (1985)

Engine	Watercooled 16-valve DOHC 72-degree V4
Capacity	1198cc
Claimed power	143bhp at 8000rpm
Weight	270kg (595lbs) wet
Top speed	140mph (224km/h)
Standing quarter-mile	11.5sec/123mph (197km/h)

YAMAHA VMX1200 V-MAX

There has never been another bike quite like the mighty Yamaha VMX1200, and there probably never will be. Big, blunt and brutally powerful, the V-Max was Yamaha's attempt at building an out-and-out musclebike: a Japanese-manufactured two-wheeled equivalent of the traditional American street rods, with their big-inch engines and asphalt-tearing acceleration so beloved by US racers.

It certainly had the horsepower. The V-Max's water-cooled, 1198cc V4 motor kicked-out 143bhp to make this by some distance the world's most powerful production motor-cycle. It had the looks, too: dramatic, cut-down styling centred on the massive engine, with fake air-scoops jutting out from either side of a dummy fuel tank. The V-Max didn't have much of a chassis – but to some riders that merely added to the attraction.

This bike was all about its powerplant, a 72-degree shaft-drive V4 borrowed from the Venture tourer. Yamaha's engineers tuned the Venture's 95bhp, 16-valve engine with conventional hot-rodding ingredients including high-lift cams, big valves, lightened pistons and toughened crank-shaft. Then they added V-boost, an ingenious system that linked the carburetors to provide extra mixture – and instant extra power – at high revs.

The result was stunning speed from a bike whose high, wide bars and upright riding position were better suited to laid-back cruising. Accelerate hard from the lights, and the V-Max hurtled away leaving a thick black line on the asphalt from its world's widest 150 × 15in rear tire. Crack the throttle at 50mph in top gear, and the Yamaha wrenched your shoulders from their sockets as it accelerated harder than anything on the road.

That performance was remarkable because at almost 600lbs the Max was far heavier than most superbikes – and far more clumsy. Adding the VMX's power and weight to a chassis containing heavily raked forks and unsophisticated twin shocks produced an ungainly, slow-steering bike that could easily become a real handful in bends.

All of which made it doubly ironic that the Yamaha was eventually sold in some legislation-conscious European countries, including Britain and France, with its engine detuned to a mere 95bhp. Remove the magnificent excess of its motor, and there wasn't much left of the V-Max.

Left: An awesome V-twin engine was the centerpiece of the V-Max in every respect. Airscoops alongside the petrol tank were fake, but the Yamaha's menacing look was very genuine.

Far left: The V-Max's natural habitat was the drag-strip, where there were no bends to show-up its handling, and the motor's explosive straight-line speed could be used to the full.

SUZUKI GSX-R1100

The format was obvious, following the introduction of the GSX-R750 a year earlier, but the brilliance of Suzuki's GSX-R1100 still took the breath away. To the 750's considerable attributes of speed, lightness, handling and braking, the 1100 added the midrange punch that only a large-capacity engine could provide. The result was the fastest and simply the *best* sports bike yet produced.

In looks and intent there was nothing new about the 'Eleven,' which shared the smaller model's endurance-racer styling, plus its oilcooled engine and alloy frame technology. But the new bike's 1052cc motor, a development of Suzuki's faithful aircooled, 16-valve GSX1100 engine, combined a maximum output of 125bhp with an enormously wide spread of power.

Its chassis was very similar to that of the 1986 GSX-R750, with its lengthened swing arm; the bigger bike was also fitted with a steering damper for extra stability. Forks were identical but the rear shock was new, the 18-inch wheels and tires wider, and the brake discs larger. Total weight was 45lbs up on the 750 at 433lbs dry, still amazingly light for an open-class machine.

Never before had such a dazzling engine been coupled with so little weight and such a competent chassis. The GSX-R annihilated the standing quarter-mile in under 11 seconds – by some distance the fastest ever – on the way to a top speed of 155mph. It had power everywhere, in marked contrast to the peaky 750. The Eleven pulled crisply from as

low as 3000rpm, and was thrillingly fast everywhere from 5000rpm to the redline at 10,500rpm.

Fine handling also contributed to the ease with which the GSX-R could be ridden fast. Steering was neutral and precise, stability impeccable, tires and brakes excellent. The twin-headlamp fairing combined with the crouched-forward riding position to give good wind protection even at the speeds the GSX-R encouraged.

The Suzuki's uncompromising nature made it uncomfortable for the rider at slow speed, and for a pillion at any speed. But its blend of power, lightness and handling had not been approached before. As an out-and-out sportster, the GSX-R1100 was in a class of its own.

SUZUKI GSX-R1100 (1986)

Engine	Oilcooled 16-valve DOHC transverse four
Capacity	1052cc
Claimed power	125bhp at 8500rpm
Weight	197kg (433lbs) dry
Top speed	155mph (248km/h)
Standing quarter-mile	10.9sec/126mph (202km/h)

Left: Styling was almost identical to that of the GSX-R750, but the Eleven's added midrange power made it much faster and easier to ride.

Above: Superb handling and generous ground-clearance contributed to the Suzuki's unmatched ability as a sportster.

Above left: Responsive motor and light weight made lifting the front wheel delightfully easy.

HONDA VFR750F

Few new models have been as important to their manufacturers as the VFR750 was to Honda in 1986. Three years earlier their first V4 sportster, the VF750, had been greeted by widespread acclaim – only to find the cheers turning to jeers as its motor proved disastrously unreliable. Those problems, plus competition from Suzuki's GSX-R750 and Yamaha's FZ750, meant Honda's next 750 had to be good.

The VFR750 was more than just good. After coming very close to abandoning the V4 concept, Honda persevered – and with the VFR they produced a masterpiece. The newcomer rapidly proved its reliability and became hugely popular thanks to its addictive blend of power delivery and handling.

Its watercooled, 90-degree V4 engine was closely based on the VF's, but incorporated numerous detail changes including gear drive to the twin overhead cams, and a 180-degree crankshaft (each pair of pistons moving in opposite directions) instead of the VF's 360-degree layout. The 748cc, 16-valve motor's dimensions were unchanged but lighter valves, pistons and conrods helped push peak power to 105bhp at 10,500rpm.

The Honda's chassis followed Suzuki's lead in using an aluminum main frame, in this case with a steel rear subframe. Air-assisted forks held a 16-inch front wheel, while the single shock benefited from a remote preload adjuster. Riding position was roomy, and the full fairing was finished in sober dark blue or white to emphasize the VFR's position as an all-rounder.

Few who rode the Honda needed much convincing that it thoroughly deserved the description. The VFR was quick, with a top speed of around 150mph. But more importantly, its instant midrange response and smooth, free-flowing power delivery gave a wonderfully relaxed ride.

Handling backed it up, combining easy steering with reassuring stability. Suspension was slightly soft for ultra-hard riding, and the seat was not soft enough. But the efficient fairing helped make the Honda comfortable enough to take long distances in its stride.

Two years later the VFR was subtly updated with a 17-inch front wheel, more protective fairing and new suspension. By then Honda's problems were over. The VFR750 had become regarded as the best all-round motorbike money could buy, and the new model did nothing to change that view.

Right: Honda's great all-rounder was equally at home whether touring, trickling through traffic or – as here – scratching round a racetrack bend.

HONDA VFR750F (1986)

Engine	Watercooled 16-valve DOHC 90-degree V4
Capacity	748cc
Claimed power	105bhp at 10,500rpm
Weight	198kg (436lbs) dry
Top speed	148mph (237km/h)
Standing quarter-mile	11.7sec/118mph (189km/h)

BIMOTA DB1

Above: DB1's compact Ducati V-twin engine and minimalist kept frame weight to a minimum.

Right: Sculpted fairing/ petrol tank/seat assembly made the Bimota a beautiful motorbike.

Utterly gorgeous from the tip of its screen to the tailpiece of its curvaceous fairing/tank/seat unit, Bimota's DB1 would demand inclusion in any list of the world's most handsome motorcycles. That it was not only an exciting bike but also a hugely important one seems almost a bonus, but the DB1 is the machine on which Bimota's current prosperity is based.

When the DB1 was released in 1986, the little firm from the Italian resort of Rimini was in deep financial trouble. Despite an unmatched reputation for exotic sportsters built around Japanese engines and their own high-quality frames, Bimota sales had been hit by advances in Japanese chassis technology.

Chief engineer Federico Martini's response was to combine Bimota's chassis expertise with a 750cc V-twin engine from nearby Ducati. The resultant all-Italian image gave the DB1 instant appeal. So too did Martini's stunning bodywork, which wrapped almost the entire bike in a streamlined fiberglass shell.

Ducati's engine was the familiar 90-degree aircooled V-twin, as fitted to the Bologna firm's F1 model. That meant belt drive to single overhead camshafts, with desmodromic valvegear. The motor acted as a stressed member of a steel ladder frame, similar in type to the standard production Ducati trellis.

Naturally the frame was immaculately constructed and fitted with premium Italian cycle parts. Marzocchi supplied the shock and forks, the latter incorporating unusual remote reservoirs of dubious benefit but undoubted appeal. Brakes were Brembo's finest, bolted to 16-inch wheels wearing Pirelli's new low-profile radial tires.

The tiny Bimota's weight of only 354lbs helped give rapid

acceleration, although the Ducati engine's 76bhp output did not let the DB1 match Japanese sportsters in a straight line. With its rider tucked tight behind the low screen, the free-breathing Bimota roared to about 130mph. Handling was predictably nimble and precise despite suspension that was too stiff to work well on anything other than a smooth surface. Given the right road, the DB1's agility and brilliant brakes meant it could match bikes with far more power.

Ultimately, however, the DB1's most important success was not on road or track but in the showroom. Its instant worldwide popularity solved Bimota's financial problems and laid the foundation for many great bikes to come.

BIMOTA DB1 (1986)

Engine	Aircooled 4-valve SOHC desmodromic 90-degree V-twin
Capacity	748cc
Claimed power	76bhp at 9000rpm
Weight	161kg (354lbs) dry
Top speed	130mph (208km/h)
Standing quarter-mile	12sec/105mph (168km/h)

HONDA CBR1000F

The CBR1000 represented a triumph for the pragmatists over the romantics in the offices of the world's largest motorcycle manufacturer. Honda's new superbike could have been a bigger version of the VFR750, an ultimate expression of the alloy-framed V4 concept they so admired. But the bean-counters decreed that things should be kept simple and cheap with a steel-framed in-line four, and the CBR was the result.

Its 998cc engine was unremarkable in design: a twin-cam, 16-valve unit with a central camchain, gear-driven balancer shaft and alternator above the five-speed gearbox. Its performance, though, was anything but. The maximum power output of 133bhp was matched by equally strong torque throughout the range. This mighty motor lived beneath bulbous, all-enveloping bodywork that resulted in the CBR being dubbed motorcycling's Ford Sierra. The plastic also hid the box-section steel frame, which held air-assisted forks and a preload-adjustable monoshock.

The package was far from a demonstration of Honda's technical expertise, but the prosaic CBR was nevertheless hugely impressive as a fast, comfortable and practical sportster. Its engine was supremely smooth, had plenty of midrange grunt and kicked again at the top end to send the slippery CBR to a genuine 160mph top speed.

Handling was respectable, with no real vices although the Honda's near-500lbs weight and conservative steering geometry gave it a ponderous feel in slow bends. The screen was too low to be of much use at speed, but the generous seat was some compensation.

In most respects the CBR outperformed Kawasaki's popular GPZ1000RX, its closest rival – just as Honda had intended. It sold well for two years before being superseded in 1989 by the 1000F-K, whose most obvious difference was restyled bodywork with a more pointed, aggressive front section.

The new fairing gave better protection, and was backed-up by a host of detail changes. The engine's crankshaft and alternator were lightened, and the lump was lowered in an otherwise unchanged frame. New forks were backed-up by wider 17-inch wheels and tires.

The improvements were small, but they made the CBR1000 slightly more responsive, nimble and comfortable – an even better long-distance rocketship than ever.

HONDA CBR1000F (1987)	
Engine	Watercooled 16-valve DOHC transverse four
Capacity	998cc
Claimed power	133bhp at 10,000rpm
Weight	222kg (488lbs) dry
Top speed	160mph (256km/h)
Standing quarter-mile	11.2sec/125mph (200km/h)

Right: Honda's all-enveloping bodywork gave distinctive looks and made engine appearance unimportant.

Inset: The big CBR was heavy and rather ponderous, but it could still be ridden respectably rapidly when required.

YAMAHA FZR1000

Yamaha's entry in the big-bore super sports battle arrived late, but it did so at speed and in style. The FZR1000 was launched in 1987, a year after Suzuki's GSX-R1100. In almost every respect, the two bikes were so closely matched that splitting them was no easy task.

The FZR had been eagerly awaited for some time, and consisted of an enlarged FZ750 motor in a chassis based on that of Yamaha's 'Genesis' factory racebike. Its centerpiece was the Deltabox frame, a rigid aluminum structure whose thick main beams ran almost directly from steering head to swingarm pivot.

The angled-forward cylinders of Yamaha's 20-valve engine were ideally suited to the layout. The watercooled motor was enlarged to 989cc, but clever design meant the cylinder block was no wider than the 750's, and the pistons and conrods were lighter. Claimed output of 125bhp neatly matched that of the GSX-R1100.

Cycle parts were conventional, with the 41mm forks and rear monoshock adjustable only for preload. Front wheel was 17 inches in diameter and, like the 18-inch rear, wore low-profile radial rubber. The rider, crouched behind a twin-headlamp full fairing, had a very long reach forward to low clip-ons.

The Yamaha was a singleminded motorbike with a gem of an engine. Smooth and torquey, it would pull from as little as 2000rpm in top gear. Power grew ferociously, with just a slight hesitation around 5000rpm, until the FZR was screaming toward the redline at close to 160mph. The chassis was equally good, combining unerring stability with remarkable agility for a liter bike. Brakes were eyeball-poppingly power

ful; the fat radials sticky. Predictable sportsbike drawbacks regarding comfort and practicality applied, but for hard riding the FZR was magnificent.

Whether it was better than the GSX-R1100 was another matter. The slightly lighter Suzuki perhaps had the edge on acceleration; the smaller Yamaha on top speed. The FZR, with its racer chassis geometry and smaller front wheel, was more maneuverable, which perhaps just gave it the edge. The battle was very close, but one thing was for sure. The FZR1000 had brought Yamaha to the forefront of superbike design.

YAMAHA FZR1000 (1987)

Engine	Watercooled 20-valve DOHC transverse four
Capacity	989cc
Claimed power	125bhp at 10,000rpm
Weight	204kg (448lbs) dry
Top speed	158mph (253km/h)
Standing quarter-mile	11sec/126mph (202km/h)

Below: Rear view was all that most got of the FZR1000, when only Suzuki's GSX-R1100 was in the same league.

Right: Light steering, near-flawless stability and grippy tires meant the Yamaha's handling was impressive.

HONDA CBR600F

The term superbike was coined to describe the biggest and fastest bikes on the road, but engineering advances in the Eighties brought a new class into the picture. Four-cylinder middleweights developed to become genuine pocket rockets – fast, manageable and exciting. The best of the bunch was Honda's CBR600.

Comparing the CBR with Honda's original CB750 showed that the 600 was 12bhp more powerful and 100lbs lighter than its 18-year-old predecessor. With a top speed of nearly 140mph, it was also over 10mph faster. It was more comfortable, and had far better handling, brakes and tires.

In reality the CBR owed some inspiration to Honda's 1975-model CB400/4, the original 'poor boy's musclebike,' and more to Kawasaki's GPZ600 four, which had been a bestseller since its introduction in 1985. The CBR600, like its 1000cc brother, targeted Kawasaki and scored a direct hit.

Visually and technically similar to the CBR1000F, the smaller model housed a 598cc watercooled, 16-valve in-line four in a steel frame. Its class-leading output of 85bhp arrived at 11,000rpm, revealing a rev-happy nature. Cycle parts were simple in specification but adequate in practice, giving the little CBR poise as well as pace.

The 600 had little of the 1000's low and midrange torque, but went like a bullet provided the tacho needle was kept above about 7000rpm by frequent use of the six-speed gearbox. Smaller dimensions, less weight and similar 17-inch wheels made the 600 much more agile.

To the CBR1000's drawback of a low screen the 600 added a small 3.7-gallon petrol tank. But in most respects it was a superbly capable all-rounder, and met Honda's aim to provide performance at the right price. Predictably, it was soon top of the sales charts.

Two years later the CBR was tuned slightly to give 93bhp, but the major revision came in 1991 when almost every component was modified to make the CBR sharper and more powerful. It now produced 100bhp at a sky-high 12,000rpm, giving a top speed of very nearly 150mph. The figures had changed; the conclusion hadn't. Middleweight or not, the Honda CBR600F was still every inch of a truly first-rate and dynamic superbike.

Above: The revamped 1991-model CBR was better-looking, more agile and faster than ever, with a top speed approaching 150mph.

HONDA CBR600F (1987)

Engine	Watercooled 16-valve DOHC transverse four
Capacity	598cc
Claimed power	85bhp at 11,000rpm
Weight	182kg (401lbs) dry
Top speed	137mph (219km/h)
Standing quarter-mile	12.2sec/115mph (184km/h)

Left: The smaller CBR had similar styling to its bigger, 1000cc brother – not to mention very respectable all-round performance of its own.

HONDA RC30

Above: Honda's brilliantly evocative RC30: every serious street-racer's ultimate fantasy.

For years it had been the serious street-racer's ultimate fantasy: the chance to ride a factory racebike on the road. Then Honda released the VFR750R, codenamed RC30, and suddenly the impossible dream had come true – provided you had the money.

Much more than simply a race-replica, the RC30 was outrageously close to being a carbon copy of Honda's works RVF750, the V4 that had dominated Formula One and endurance racing throughout the mid-Eighties. Hand-built in limited numbers and crammed with lightweight components, the RC30 was the most exotic Honda roadster yet.

Its layout mimicked the RVF from its tiny dimensions, twin-headlamp fairing and single seat to the alloy twin-beam frame, which was rumored to be cast in the same dies as the racebike's. The rear wheel was held by Honda's single-sided Pro Arm, as pioneered by the innovative Elf racers and fitted to the RVF endurance bikes to save time on tire-changes.

Many experts disputed Honda's claim that the Pro Arm was more rigid than conventional swing-arms of the same weight, but the right-side view of the RC30's apparently unsuspended rear wheel was undeniably striking. Suspension was conventional but highly sophisticated, contributing to a price which was almost double that of the standard VFR750F.

The RC motor was basically a tuned and slimmed-down version of the standard VFR's 748cc V4 lump. It used a 360-degree crankshaft (pairs of pistons rising and falling together), like the RVF and the earlier VF750 roadster, because

this gave better drive out of corners than the 180-degree VFR750F set-up.

Bigger carbs, a revised valve-train, more compression and titanium conrods helped the Honda produce 112bhp at 11,000rpm. But more than sheer power, it was the peerless combination of low size and weight, razor-sharp handling, brilliant brakes and growling V4 torque that made the RC30 virtually unbeatable in production-based racing.

As a streetbike the RC was compromised by its radical riding position, thinly padded single seat and the close-ratio gearbox's high first ratio – good for 80mph! But on the right road it was wonderful: lightning fast, supremely responsive and, above all, thrillingly evocative of the legendary RVF that it so closely resembled.

HONDA RC30 (1988)

Engine	Watercooled 16-valve DOHC 90-degree V4
Capacity	748cc
Claimed power	112bhp at 11,000rpm
Weight	185kg (407lbs) dry
Top speed	155mph (248km/h)
Standing quarter-mile	12.2sec/120mph (192km/h)

DUCATI 851

Above: The sophisticated, eight-valve 851; leading Ducati toward an exciting future.

Ducati's reputation for building high-class sporting V-twins gained a new dimension with the arrival of the 851. The Italian factory's bikes had traditionally been thundering air-cooled devices, high on handling and charisma but short on sophistication. The watercooled 851, with its four-valve cylinder heads and advanced fuel-injection system, signalled a new era for the famous old firm from Bologna.

Chief engineer Massimo Bordi was determined to create an eight-valve desmo twin, something his legendary predecessor Fabio Taglioni had always resisted. The resultant design retained the trademark 90-degree cylinder angle. But watercooling, Weber-Marelli injection and the new cylinder heads' improved breathing allowed a 100bhp output that made this the most powerful Ducati yet.

The 851cc motor was a stressed member of the traditional Ducati ladder frame of narrow steel tubes, which held cycle parts including top-notch Marzocchi suspension and Brembo brakes. The rounded full fairing and single seat were finished in a patriotic paint scheme of red, white and green.

Crisp, smooth and refined, the engine combined Ducati's famous V-twin torque with an exhilarating top-end rush, giving a top speed of almost 150mph. But problems of supply meant the original, '88-model 851 was fitted with 16-inch wheels, instead of the 17-inchers it should have worn. Handling was decidedly strange, and the 851's reception was mixed.

All that changed a year later, when a revamped bike, clad in Italian racing red, emerged to reveal the full brilliance of the 851's basic design. Engine changes included a revised fuel-injection system, new cams and increased compression, giving a total of 104bhp. More importantly, the frame was slightly modified, the shock was new – and the 851 wore the 17-inch wheels it should have had all along.

The result was a transformed bike with gorgeous looks, breathtaking performance and the lovely, free-flowing feel that only a big V-twin can provide. The new 851 was super-fast, impeccably balanced and wonderfully surefooted; its rigid, lavishly equipped chassis now a perfect match for the potent eight-valve engine. On top of all that, the 851's neat finish and aura of sheer class confirmed that this was the bike that would lead Ducati toward an exciting future in the motorcycling business.

DUCATI 851 (1989)

Engine	Watercooled 8-valve DOHC desmodromic 90-degree V-twin
Capacity	851cc
Claimed power	104bhp at 9000rpm
Weight	180kg (396lbs) dry
Top speed	150mph (240km/h)
Standing quarter-mile	11.5sec/118mph (189km/h)

BMW K1

Of all the world's manufacturers, German traditionalists BMW were about the least likely to produce a super sports bike with futuristic styling and eyecatching graphics. But that's exactly what they did in 1989, with the release of the big, bright and exceptionally bold K1.

From a firm that specialized in conservative tourers, the newcomer's aerodynamic lines and hard-edged nature were startling. But BMW had decided that their image needed a lift, and the K1 – featuring a tuned version of the four-cylinder K100 engine in a new chassis – was the result. Its slippery shape, which stretched from the semi-enclosed front wheel to the strangely bulging tailpiece, was a result of BMW's decision to build, for worldwide consumption, a sportster governed by Germany's 100bhp power limit. When giving away 20bhp or more to the opposition, the low 0.34cd drag coefficient was an important performance aid.

Those 100 horses came from a 16-valve version of BMW's watercooled, 987cc motor which, with its horizontal cylinders set along the line of the bike, had been introduced five years earlier in the K100. A new engine-management system, increased compression and lightened crankshaft boosted power by 10 percent, and torque by more.

The K1 wore Marzocchi forks and Brembo brakes from Italy, with optional anti-lock. The single rear shock benefited from Paralever – a system of rods, developed on BMW's trail bikes, that reduced the drive shaft's traditional adverse effect on handling.

BMW's blaster had few equals for traveling long distances fast. Top speed was close to 150mph, with crisp response throughout the range. The efficient fairing, comfortable riding position and excellent fuel economy made rapid cruising temptingly easy, too. And although the K1 was long and heavy, its firm suspension, stable handling and powerful brakes were a revelation.

The German bike lacked the speed and agility of a true sportster, and for touring was marred by its annoying inability to carry a pillion and luggage simultaneously, though panniers were belatedly made available in 1992. But the K1 was quick, comfortable and striking. Its futuristic image was good for BMW, and so was its up-to-date engineering – especially in later years, when much K1 technology filtered down to other models.

BMW K1 (1989)

Engine	Watercooled 16-valve DOHC longitudinal four
Capacity	987cc
Claimed power	100bhp at 8000rpm
Weight	234kg (468lbs) wet
Top speed	145mph (232km/h)
Standing quarter-mile	12sec/117mph (187km/h)

Above left: Futuristic shapes, bright colors and bold graphics were a radical departure for traditionally conservative BMW.

Above: Styling was that of a pure sportster, but the big, relatively mild K1 excelled as a relaxed, high-mileage sports-tourer.

KAWASAKI ZXR750

Kawasaki opted for the straightforward approach when they belatedly decided to build a 750cc race-replica. They modified their existing four-cylinder engine, put it in an alloy, twin-beam frame and attached some serious cycle parts. Then they added a full fairing with a menacing, racetrack-inspired paint scheme, and named their creation the ZXR750.

The motor was a much-reworked version of the GPX750's watercooled, 16-valve unit, with bigger valves, higher compression ratio and a lightened crankshaft. Surprisingly, its peak output of 105bhp at 10,500rpm was barely up on that of the GPX. Despite the ZXR's alloy frame and racy look, at 452lbs it was also slightly heavier than the steel-framed GPX roadster, let alone lightweight rivals such as Suzuki's GSX-R. But the Kawasaki's frame was hugely strong, backed-up by big disc brakes and wide, radial-tired 17-inch wheels.

Styling was inspired. Futuristic air-ducts swept back from the nose of the neat twin-headlamp fairing, with its bold stripes of either red/black or blue/white/green. The ZXR was undoubtedly built to a price, but it looked a million dollars.

As a roadster it was quite quick enough, too, combining a genuine 150mph top speed with an aggressive riding position and a chassis that was as happy on the racetrack as on the street. The engine made good top-end power, brakes were superb and handling was taut and stable, though marred by slow steering and a firm rear shock. The ZXR was not the fastest of the super sports 750s, and it wasn't the lightest or most agile. But its instant popularity proved that lacking the last few percent of performance didn't matter if the style and price were right.

A year later, in 1990, the ZXR was revamped with slightly more power and less weight. 1991 saw a comprehensive redesign featuring a shorter-stroke engine with its camchain on the end of the block. Chassis mods included a lighter frame with shorter wheelbase, steeper steering geometry and upside-down forks.

The changes worked, giving the Kawasaki a crisper engine response (although power output was back down to 100bhp) and much lighter, more precise handling. At last, the ZXR750 was as fast and as furious as it looked.

KAWASAKI ZXR750 (1989)

Engine	Watercooled 16-valve DOHC transverse four
Capacity	748cc
Claimed power	105bhp at 10,500rpm
Weight	205kg (452lbs) dry
Top speed	150mph (240km/h)
Standing quarter-mile	11.4sec/120mph (192km/h)

Left: Firmly suspended and built for speed, the ZXR was at its best when being ridden as fast as possible.

Insert: A stylish paint scheme and neat touches like the air-duct gave the ZXR visual appeal.

BUELL RS1200

The idea of a racy Harley-Davidson has long appealed to riders captivated by the thundering Milwaukee V-twins. But not, it seems, to the Harley factory bosses, who since the failure of the XLCR1000 Cafe Racer seemed content to release nothing more aggressive than cruisers and full-dress tourers.

Enter Erik Buell, a former road-racer and Harley engineer who set up a small firm in Mukwanago, Wisconsin, to produce a Harley-engined cafe racer of his own. His first effort, the RR1000, created much interest and was successful in twin-cylinder racing, but it was with his second model, the RS1200, that Buell hit the mark.

Unlike the fully faired and rather anonymous looking RR, the RS had a half-fairing that kept Harley's distinctive 45-degree V-twin motor – in this case a 1200cc Sportster unit – in view. And it also revealed much more of the innovative, high-quality engineering that made the RS special.

Buell's frame was a Ducati-style ladder of thin steel tubes, which held the engine via an ingenious rubber-mounting system. Forks were Italian Marzocchi units modified with Erik's own anti-dive system; rear suspension an unusual design based around a single shock placed horizontally below the engine.

Even the 17-inch wheels and four-piston front brake calipers were Buell's own work, as was the distinctive fiberglass

bodywork. The neat fairing/tank/tailpiece unit featured a seat hump which was hinged to become a back-rest for the pillion.

Numerous tuning parts were available for Harley engines but in standard form, modified only by a SuperTrapp exhaust, the 1200cc Evolution Sportster motor made about 70bhp. That was enough to push the Buell to around 120mph, with plenty of V-twin grunt at low revs and very little of the standard Sportster's vibration.

The RS1200's short wheelbase and steep steering geometry meant it handled like no standard Harley. Steering was delightfully easy and precise, marred only by a slight lack of control from the underslung shock. The RS more than lived-up to Buell's slogan of 'America's Faaast Motorcycle.'

Inevitably, the RS1200 was expensive, costing more than twice as much as a standard Sportster. It was also stylish, in-

BUELL RS1200 (1989)

Engine	Aircooled 4-valve pushrod 45-degree V-twin
Capacity	1200cc
Claimed power	70bhp at 5000rpm
Weight	205kg (450lbs) dry
Top speed	122mph (195km/h)
Standing quarter-mile	13.5sec/100mph (160km/h)

novative and beautifully crafted – a fine attempt at building a true Harley sports bike.

Left: Stylish and beautifully engineered, the RS1200 proved that it *was* possible to build a serious sports bike around Harley-Davidson's legendary V-twin powerplant.

Above: The Buell's half-fairing had the advantage of leaving the distinctive rubber-mounted Sportster motor, and the horizontal shock absorber mounted below it, on show.

YAMAHA FZR600

Yamaha didn't have far to look for inspiration when they decided to build a new 600cc sportster for 1989. They already had a sharp-handling 600, the FZ, whose aircooled engine was becoming increasingly uncompetitive. And they had a range of modern watercooled fours in sizes of 1000, 750 and 400cc. Equipping the FZ600 with a new watercooled engine would have made quite a bike, but Yamaha went further: the FZR600's frame was a twin-spar Deltabox design and the front wheel size was increased to 17 inches.

But not many, for the FZR was built strictly to a price. Its frame was steel instead of the FZR1000's aluminum, its forks were skinny, non-adjustable units and the shock was tuneable only for preload. The lean, mean (in both senses) FZR incorporated few of the neat touches of some rivals. Its 599cc engine contained 16 valves, instead of 20 like the bigger

Above: Built for budget-priced superbike thrills, the FZR600 encouraged an aggressive riding style – and its chassis was normally good enough to let you get away with it.

Above right: Styling was purposely similar to that of

Yamaha's FZR1000 flagship, but the 600 lacked the bigger bike's midrange muscle, alloy frame and sophisticated cycle parts.

Right: Light weight, racy riding position and a well-balanced chassis meant the FZR could compete well.

lumps, because Yamaha claimed five-valve technology was unnecessary with small cylinders. The 600 lacked the FZR1000's new EXUP exhaust valve, too, although its high 12:1 compression ratio helped give a competitive 90bhp.

The FZR600 was a charger, built for high-speed, low-budget thrills with little thought given to comfort. It was small and sparsely furnished, with low bars, high pegs and a thinly padded seat. In best middleweight tradition it required plenty of rider involvement to produce its best.

Performance was lazy below 7000rpm but above that figure the FZR took off, screaming to 140mph provided the rider crouched behind the excellent fairing, and kept stirring the six-speed gearbox. The motor was reasonably smooth and the FZR's raw, revvy nature added to the excitement. Suspension was slightly crude but the Yamaha's frame was rigid, the geometry was just right and the FZR went round corners with all but the most agile. It was light, its brakes were good and on a twisty road it was arguably the best of the middleweights.

Two years later it was improved slightly with a sharper fairing, wider rear wheel and radial tyres. By then the competition had moved on, and Honda's CBR was in most respects a better bike. But for pure sports riding, the FZR600 still took some beating.

YAMAHA FZR600 (1989)

Engine	Watercooled 16-valve DOHC transverse four
Capacity	599cc
Claimed power	90bhp at 10,500rpm
Weight	179kg (394lbs) dry
Top speed	140mph (224km/h)
Standing quarter-mile	12sec/110mph (176km/h)

KAWASAKI ZZ-R1100

At the start of the Nineties, Kawasaki's reputation for powerful fours stretched back almost 20 years to the Z1 – but even so, the sheer brute force of the ZZ-R1100 took the breath away. The watercooled, 1052cc engine was a monster of a powerplant whose 145bhp gave the ZZ-R ferocious acceleration to a genuine top speed of 175mph. The ZZ-R1100 had many other attributes, for it was a very refined and competent sports-touring motorcycle. But the centerpiece of the whole bike, the thing that made the ZZ-R special, was its incredible engine.

Based on the watercooled, 16-valve unit of the 1988-model ZX-10 (and owing much to the 900R of four years earlier), the ZZ-R motor contained bigger valves, lighter pistons and much strengthening. But the vital introduction was the ram-air system, based on Formula One car technology, which ducted air from a slot in the fairing (below the headlight) directly to the airbox.

The system was sealed, so the faster the Kawasaki went, the more cool air was forced down the gaping 40mm carbs into the engine. The result was sensational. At low revs the ZZ-R was smooth and pleasantly tractable. And from about 6000rpm, when it breathed deeper and really went to work, it was viciously, thrillingly powerful – simply in a different league to anything else on the road.

Happily, this mighty motor was housed in a very competent chassis. The aluminum frame was based on that of the ZX-10, and held a strengthened swing arm, 43mm forks from the ZXR750, and a damping-adjustable Kayaba shock. Wheels were wide 17-inchers wearing radial tires; front brake combined 310mm discs with four-piston calipers.

Everything worked, and the ZZ-R handled very well, although Kawasaki were quick to emphasize that it was not a race-replica. That was supported not only by the bike's relatively high weight, but also by the semi-upright riding position, roomy seat and generally high level of finish.

The fairing was impressive, and the ZZ-R's smoothness and practicality earned it a reputation as a comfortable and efficient all-rounder. But, deep down, the attraction was clear. Above all, the ZZ-R1100 was searingly fast.

KAWASAKI ZZ-R1100 (1990)

Engine	Watercooled 16-valve DOHC transverse four
Capacity	1052cc
Claimed power	145bhp at 9500 rpm
Weight	228kg (502lbs) dry
Top speed	175mph (280km/h)
Standing quarter-mile	10.8sec/130mph (208km/h)

Left: The ZZ-R1100's roomy riding position and rounded, conservatively styled bodywork gave little hint of the brute strength bolted between the alloy frame spars of the world's most powerful streetbike.

Inset: Despite being big, heavy and comfortable enough to be described as a sports-tourer rather than a sports bike, the ZZ-R's rigid frame and firm, well-controlled suspension made for excellent handling.

NORTON F1

It was the howl that stayed in the memory; a smooth, high-pitched scream that ripped from twin mufflers as the Norton F1's rotary motor hit 6000rpm and surged toward the redline with renewed thrust. The F1's distinctive exhaust note emphasized that this bike was different not only from previous Nortons but also from every other sportster ever built.

The launch of the F1 in 1990 was remarkable in itself. Norton's comeback had begun a few years earlier with the release, after 15 years of rotary development, of the Classic roadster. The touring Commander followed, and public interest in Norton snowballed when enthusiastic workers built an alloy-framed rotary racer that won two national championships in 1989.

A roadgoing version was the obvious next step. The F1 was powered by a Commander engine, turned back-to-front, fitted with Mikuni carburetors and uprated with the five-speed gearbox from Yamaha's FZR1000. Enlarged ports and revised timing helped lift output from 85 to 95bhp at 9500rpm.

The frame, built by local specialists Spondon Engineering, was similar to the racebike's but stronger and had slightly more conservative steering geometry. Dutch firm White Power provided the multi-adjustable upside-down forks and shock. Brembo brakes and Michelin radials completed an upmarket package. Styling incorporated smooth bodywork that hid much of the technology but left space for the cigarette-packet logos of race-team sponsors JPS. Riding position was sporty, with wide clip-ons and a single seat.

The F1's power and weight figures were similar to those of a typical Japanese 600, and so was its 145mph top speed. On the road, the rotary felt totally different, though, thanks to its smoothness, generous midrange punch and spine-tingling high-rev howl. For a sportster, the F1 was fairly comfortable, and its rigid frame and excellent suspension gave precise, surefooted handling. But there were rough edges: the Norton was thirsty, its engine snatched at low revs and was prone to overheating, and ground clearance was poor.

The hand-built F1 was also extremely expensive, a problem Norton addressed a year later with the slightly cheaper F1 Sport, which used simpler bodywork and lower-spec cycle parts. The Sport was a little less sleek and sophisticated. But like the F1, it was quick, agile and distinctive.

NORTON F1 (1990)	
Engine	Watercooled twin-chamber rotary
Capacity	588cc
Claimed power	95bhp at 9500rpm
Weight	192g (422lbs) dry
Top speed	145mph (232km/h)
Standing quarter-mile	12.5sec/112mph (179km/h)

Above: The roadster was derived from Norton's phenomenally powerful and highly successful racing rotary, which took Steve Spray to two national championships in 1989.

Far left: The F1's rather Honda CBR-like styling was pleasingly sleek and modern, though sadly it hid the Norton's unique rotary engine from view.

Left: Small, neat and nimble, the rotary had a nominal capacity of 558cc and performance comparable with that of a typical Japanese 600cc four. Low-volume production meant the Norton's price was in a different league altogether.

HONDA VFR750FL

Sometimes even being brilliant isn't enough. In the years after its introduction, the original VFR750 transformed Honda's reputation for V4s and established itself as arguably the best balanced superbike on the road. But by 1990 it was losing sales to the race-replica 750s from Kawasaki and Suzuki, so Honda replaced it with the VFR750FL.

The VFR name remained the same, but so much was changed that the L was virtually a new bike. It was sharper and more focused than the original middle-of-the-road model. The new VFR was still no race-replica, but its body-work was sleeker and its image had been shifted subtly in that direction.

Its watercooled, 90-degree engine received many new components. Valve train was revised, camshaft gears altered, carbs enlarged, and the crankshaft made heavier. The result was a shorter, slimmer motor with a peak output of 100bhp. That was a few horses down on the old model, but midrange response was improved.

Equally importantly, the more compact motor was moved forward and down in the frame – a thicker twin-spar aluminum design like the RC30's. The steering geometry was steepened, wheelbase shortened, fork internals firmed-up and front tire widened. And the most obvious chassis mod was the adoption of an RC30-style single-sided swing-arm.

The L looked great, but whether it was better than the old model depended on what you wanted. For the all-round riding at which the VFR750 had always excelled there were definite disadvantages. In particular, the lower handlebars, shorter screen and smaller fuel tank detracted from the Honda's famed ability to handle town riding and touring. But the newcomer was better suited to a fast pace. Although the L was slightly heavier and less powerful, its meatier midrange encouraged plenty of throttle abuse. And the new bike's stiffer frame, racier geometry and better cycle parts made for sharper handling.

By no means everyone thought the L model an improvement, but in some respects Honda earned universal praise.

Instead of getting bigger and softer over the years, like so many bikes, the VFR was more lithe and handsome than ever. And for all its new muscles, the L was still far more versatile than its 750cc rivals.

HONDA VFR750FL (1990)

Engine	Watercooled 16-valve DOHC 90-degree V4
Capacity	748cc
Claimed power	100bhp at 9500rpm
Weight	216kg (475lbs) dry
Top speed	150mph (240km/h)
Standing quarter-mile	11.7sec/116mph (186km/h)

Above right: Sharper styling and a Pro-Arm single-sided swing-arm, borrowed from the RC30, shifted the VFR's image subtly for the Nineties.

Right: A thicker frame, racier steering geometry and uprated cycle-parts gave the Honda added cornering poise.

MAGNI SFIDA 1100

From the moment you fired-up the engine, the sensations were pure Moto Guzzi: the distinctive throb from twin exhaust pipes, the side-to-side rocking motion as the throttle was blipped, the view of a big aircooled cylinder head poking out from below each side of a long red fuel tank. But the name on the tank was that of another legend of Italian motorcycling – Arturo Magni.

Magni made his name as chief mechanic to the MV Agusta race team that won an incredible 17 world 500cc road-race titles in a row between 1958 and 1974. He prepared the bikes for Surtees, Hailwood, Agostini and Read. And when MV retired from racing, Arturo set up a bike business with his sons Giovanni and Carlo, near the old Agusta base at Gallarate, outside Milan.

Of their string of models, the best-known was the Sfida; the Challenge. Consisting of a big-bore Moto Guzzi engine with the Magnis' own chassis and bodywork, the Sfida combined the timeless appeal of the Mandello V-twins with increased performance and a unique style of its own.

Guzzi's 949cc Le Mans engine was tuned with a kit that raised capacity to 1105cc, and horsepower to around 90bhp. It was held in a tubular steel frame, which was similar to Guzzi's original but included an innovative 'Parallelogramo' swing-arm that reduced the shaft drive's normal adverse effect on handling. Sturdy Forcelle Italia forks, twin Koni shocks and Brembo Gold Line brakes were further classy touches. A neat half-fairing and seat unit, bright scarlet paint and spoked 18-inch wheels completed a handsome bike with the classical feel that the standard Le Mans had lost through the Eighties.

The Sfida was respectably quick, thundering up to 140mph with masses of midrange grunt available from its big, long-legged engine. Eighteen-inch wheels and conservative geometry gave impeccable stability with fairly slow steering. Suspension was firm and well-controlled; the big Brembo brakes powerful.

The Sfida had performance in plenty; but most of all it had

breeding and soul. Those great MV racers were just a memory, but Arturo Magni and his sons had ensured that the MV spirit, the spirit of great design and engineering excellence, lived on in Gallarate.

MAGNI SFIDA 1100 (1990)

Engine	Aircooled 4-valve pushrod 90-degree transverse V-twin
Capacity	1105cc
Claimed power	90bhp at 7500rpm
Weight	195kg (429lbs) dry
Top speed	140mph (224km/h)
Standing quarter-mile	13sec/110mph (176km/h)

Above: Lean, respectably agile and oozing Italian character, the Sfida was the sort of sportster that many Guzzi riders thought the Mandello factory themselves should have produced.

Left: Magni's clever Parallelogramo swing-arm gave impressive stability in bends.

BIMOTA BELLARIA

The Bellaria represented a new direction for Bimota, manufacturers of the world's most exotic big-bore sports bikes. Its capacity was a mere 600cc; its color scheme a subtle lilac instead of the normal bright reds and greens. The Bellaria was also fitted with a well-padded dual seat that made it Bimota's first bicycle made for two.

In many ways the gentle look was deceptive. The engine may have been only the watercooled, 16-valve mill from Yamaha's FZR600, but when modified by Bimota with a revised airbox and four-into-two exhaust system, it revved like crazy and made a healthy 95bhp, five horses up on standard.

More to the point, the Bellaria's chassis was closely based on that of Bimota's 750cc YB4 racebike, which had taken Virginio Ferrari to the Formula One world championship in 1987. Its frame was a twin-spar alloy construction, holding upmarket cycle parts including upside-down Marzocchi forks, wide 17-inch wheels, enormous Brembo discs and Michelin Hi-Sport radial tires.

At heart, the Bellaria was as much a sportster as any bike from Rimini. Its wheelbase was just 1375mm, fully 45mm shorter than the FZR's. Its steering geometry was racier; its weight 35lbs lower despite the Bimota rarity of a hefty alloy rear subframe carrying a pair of high-level pillion pegs.

Handlebars were slightly higher than normal, and the Bellaria combined razor-sharp handling and frantic, high-revving straight-line performance with a surprising degree of comfort. Keeping the motor buzzing above 7000rpm made for frenetic fun to 140mph plus and, unlike most Bimotas, the Bellaria was fairly happy in town or on a gentle cruise.

The Bellaria was more refined, more comfortable and even more practical than the standard FZR – not to mention faster, more agile and better braked. Unfortunately, it also cost three times as much. All that money for a mere middleweight; all that unused chassis potential, capable of harnessing half as much horsepower again.

On a value-for-money basis the Bellaria was pretty hopeless. But for riders who wanted a small Bimota, a two-seat Bimota or who simply didn't mind spending serious money for a piece of middleweight perfection, it was a very special machine indeed.

BIMOTA BELLARIA (1990)

Engine	Watercooled 16-valve DOHC transverse four
Capacity	599cc
Claimed power	95bhp at 10,500rpm
Weight	163kg (359lbs) dry
Top speed	142mph (227km/h)
Standing quarter-mile	11.5sec/112mph (179km/h)

Below: A comfortable dual-seat showed this was no typical Bimota.

Right: Middleweight engine and pillion seat or not, the Bellaria was a sporty bike.

SUZUKI GSX-R1100L

Suzuki's second-generation GSX-R1100 illustrated how it was possible to take a brilliant motorcycle and come close to spoiling it completely. The original, 1986-model GSX-R combined power and lightness with stable, forgiving handling. Its 1989 replacement, the comprehensively redesigned 1100K, was intended to be sharper and sportier – but instead turned out to be an evil-handling monster.

A year later the K was replaced by the GSX-R1100L, which was a much better bike, and worthy of its position as Suzuki's flagship. But even the L was a highly-strung beast that struggled to regain the GSX-R's reputation as the supreme Japanese sportster. Few areas were left untouched when the original oilcooled warrior was overhauled to become the faster and theoretically more maneuverable 1100K. The new bike's engine was the 75cc bigger, 1127cc lump from the GSX1100FJ sports-tourer, and developed an awesome 141bhp at 9500rpm.

But it was in the chassis that the major changes took place. There was little wrong with the new alloy frame, which was similar to the old and claimed to be stiffer, as well as shorter in the wheelbase and reworked to suit 17-inch wheels. But there was plenty wrong with ludicrously stiff suspension that made the 1100K dangerously lively on anything but a perfectly smooth road.

Suzuki acted fairly quickly to sort things out. The 1990-model 1100L held an unchanged engine in a new chassis containing upside-down forks and a new rear shock, as well as a longer swing-arm plus wider wheels and tires – the rear an enormous 180-section Michelin radial.

Suspension at both ends was multi-adjustable, with a bewildering total of literally millions of settings, of which only a minority were worth having. The Suzuki was far less forgiving than Yamaha's rival FZR1000, and many riders never got it to handle. But with perseverance the 1100L could be made to corner with great precision.

It was frighteningly fast, combining its 160mph-plus top speed with a massive midrange punch. Suzuki's missile was powerful and demanding; the maddest, baddest motorbike on the roads in 1990. The GSX-R1100L had its faults, but it sure was exciting.

SUZUKI GSX-R1100L (1990)

Engine	Oilcooled 16-valve DOHC transverse four
Capacity	1127cc
Claimed power	141bhp at 9500rpm
Weight	219kg (483lbs) dry
Top speed	165mph (264km/h)
Standing quarter-mile	10.8sec/128mph (205km/h)

YAMAHA FZR1000RU

In contrast to Suzuki's erratic attempts to modify the GSX-R1100, Yamaha's FZR1000 provided an example of how a bike could gradually be improved, in a series of well-considered steps, until its full potential was realized.

The original FZR1000 had been hugely impressive on its introduction back in 1987, but four years later the FZR was faster, nimbler, better-looking and easier to ride. Along the way it had become widely regarded as the best sports bike ever to come out of Japan.

By far the biggest change came in 1989, with the introduction of the model that became universally known as the EXUP. The name referred to an electronically operated valve in the exhaust pipe. At low revs the valve was shut, providing the engine with helpful back-pressure; at higher revs it opened to give the scavenging advantages of a long pipe.

The system added valuable midrange power, and the watercooled 20-valve motor was extensively revamped to provide gains elsewhere, too. Capacity was enlarged from 989cc to 1002cc, compression ratio increased slightly, the valve train modified to suit bigger carbs, and the five-speed gearbox redesigned.

This magnificent 140bhp motor was placed slightly more upright (cylinders 35 degrees from vertical, from 45) in a revised alloy frame. Thicker forks, a new shock, revised brake calipers, a 17-inch rear wheel and radial tires completed a comprehensively uprated chassis.

It all worked, and the EXUP brought a new dimension to supersports motorcycling. Not only was it gloriously fast, but now there was crisp, instant acceleration available almost from tickover to the 11,500rpm redline. The FZR was as stable as ever, and its new chassis gave new levels of traction and cornering control.

But Yamaha weren't finished yet, and two years later produced the FZR1000RU – recognizable by its sharper fairing which contained a single headlamp in place of the original pair. The engine and basic frame were unchanged; modifications included revised controls, a larger radiator, reworked rear subframe and upside-down forks.

The RU looked more stylish and aggressive, and if the new model was barely better than the old there was good reason for that. After all, improving on something so close to sports-bike perfection was bound to be a difficult job.

YAMAHA FZR1000RU (1991)

Engine	Watercooled 20-valve DOHC transverse four
Capacity	1002cc
Claimed power	140bhp at 10,000rpm
Weight	209kg (461lbs) dry
Top speed	168mph (269km/h)
Standing quarter-mile	10.8sec/128mph (205km/h)

Above right: Sharper nose and upside-down forks were the most obvious distinguishing marks of the FZR1000RU.

Right: Engine and frame were unchanged from the first EXUP-equipped FZR of 1989, and the 1000RU remained most pundits' choice as Japan's best big sports bike of all.

Left: With its suspension tuned correctly, the GSX-R1100L was a stunningly fast and respectably manageable motorbike.

TRIUMPH TROPHY 1200

When Britain's reborn Triumph firm launched the four-cylinder Trophy 1200 in the spring of 1991, the new bike left a trail of disbelief among those who rode it. Surely nobody could produce a debut model that was so fast, so smooth, so well-balanced, so instantly *right*.

They could. Unlikely as it had seemed, Britain's first modern superbike was a masterpiece. John Bloor, the millionaire builder who had bought bankrupt Triumph from the liquidator and secretly spent eight years developing a range of modern bikes in a purpose-built plant at Hinckley in the English Midlands, was hailed as the savior of the British motorcycle industry.

Triumph's basic watercooled engine design owed much to Japanese thinking but incorporated a modular concept unique in motorcycling. Three and four-cylinder layouts used alternative crankshafts to give four different engines and a total of six models, all using the same steel spine frame. Biggest of all was the 1200 Trophy. Its twin-cam, 16-valve motor produced a maximum of 125bhp at 9000rpm, and looked as though it could have come from Honda or Kawasaki. But although the carburetors and six-speed gearbox were Japanese, the engine was designed and built in Hinckley.

Suspension and brakes were also from Japan; the frame and many other parts were made by Triumph. With its full fairing, wide dual-seat and slightly leant-forward riding position, the Trophy was intended to compete head-on with sports-tourers such as Honda's CBR1000, Kawasaki's ZZ-R1100 and Yamaha's FJ1200.

Compete it did, thanks in no small part to a magnificent engine. It wasn't just the Trophy's 150mph-plus top speed and exceptional smoothness that were impressive. Best of all was its enormously broad spread of power, which made the excellent six-speed gearbox almost redundant.

Handling was very adequate, despite the rather old-fashioned chassis design, combining neutral steering with suspension that provided a good compromise between comfort and control. The fairing worked well, and the 5.5 gallon fuel tank gave a generous range.

Against all the odds, the Trophy 1200 was a triumph in more than just name. Even the most cynical rider had to admit that the British motorcycle industry had been reborn in style.

TRIUMPH TROPHY 1200 (1991)

Engine	Watercooled 16-valve DOHC transverse four
Capacity	1180cc
Claimed power	125bhp at 9000rpm
Weight	240kg (529lbs) dry
Top speed	153mph (245km/h)
Standing quarter-mile	11.4sec/124mph (198km/h)

Above left: The Trophy at speed. For a debut model, the Triumph's speed, civility and sheer competitiveness with the best from Japan were hard to believe.

Above: Large-diameter steel spine frame, shared by all six of 1991's new Triumph models, looked old-fashioned but worked extremely well.

Right: Styling was criticized by some for being conservative and too closely modeled on the Japanese. Kawasaki influence was apparent in shape, engine and chassis design, but rumours of links between the two firms proved unfounded.

DUCATI 900SS

Like the 851 before it, the 900SS was a Ducati that deserved the description 'right second time.' In 1989, at the same time that they redesigned the eight-valve 851 to good effect, Ducati introduced a new V-twin whose single-cam four-valve engine and simpler chassis provided a cheaper introduction to Bolognese superbiking.

The new 900SS had much of the rugged simplicity of its great Seventies namesake, but had too many of the old charger's rough edges as well. Unadventurous styling and annoying details, especially a spluttery twin-choke Weber carburetor and crude Marzocchi suspension, ensured the 900 made little impact.

Two years later the bike was restyled and subtly modified – and suddenly Ducati found themselves with a winner. Looking much more like the 851, the '91-model SS was red, hot and handsome. Packing a crisper engine in an equally light and more responsive chassis, it epitomized everything that had been good about Ducati's raw V-twin sportsters.

DUCATI 900SS (1991)	
Engine	Air/oilcooled 4-valve SOHC desmodromic 90-degree V-twin
Capacity	904cc
Claimed power	73bhp at 7000rpm
Weight	183kg (403lbs) dry
Top speed	140mph (224km/h)
Standing quarter-mile	11.9sec/115mph (184km/h)

Above: Stylish, simple and effective, the 900SS proved – as its namesake had in the Seventies – that good looks, light weight and V-twin punch were every bit as valuable to a sports bike as sheer horsepower.

Right: The appearance of Japanese Showa suspension components alongside the traditional steel ladder frame surprised many Ducati enthusiasts, but few argued after they'd ridden the bike.

Internally the 904cc engine was unchanged. Based on the motor from the Paso sports-tourer, and cooled by a combination of air to the two-valve desmo heads and oil to the barrels, the SS produced an unchanged maximum of 73bhp at 7000rpm. (Ducatis' performance was by now measured at the rear wheel instead of the crankshaft, giving lower figures than before.) But crucially, the 44mm twin-choke Weber carburetor was replaced by a pair of 38mm downdraft Mikunis from Japan.

Japanese involvement also benefited the chassis. Suspension comprised multi-adjustable Showa units at both ends: thick upside-down forks plus a monoshock which, like the previous model's, used no rising-rate linkage. The steel ladder frame gained steeper steering geometry, and the 17-inch front wheel carried bigger, 320mm brake discs.

The revised 900SS was every bit as good as it looked. With a top speed of 140mph, its straight-line performance was barely that of a 750cc Japanese race-replica. But the Ducati's carburation was now spot-on, and the big V-twin's generous midrange power made the 900 a delightfully easy machine to ride fast.

In bends, the Duke's rigid frame, superb suspension and weight of only 400lbs made it wonderfully agile. On a twisty road, few bikes could stay with the 900SS. And none could match the V-twin's addictive blend of poise, noise and punchy power delivery.

GOODMAN HDS1200

The sound could only come from a Harley-Davidson: a low, machine-gun like bellow from shiny double-barreled mufflers. But the bike was no Harley – other senses told you that. The riding position was too sporty; the feel under hard acceleration too smooth. And the look was a unique mixture of American V-twin and Fifties British cafe-racer.

This was the Goodman HDS1200, short for Harley-Davidson Special. Designed and built by Goodman Engineering, a small English firm whose boss Simon Goodman came from the family that founded Velocette, it comprised a 1200 Sportster engine, Norton Featherbed-style frame, and a selection of serious cycle parts.

The HDS sprang from Goodman Engineering's production of replicas of the Featherbed. When Simon Goodman decided to build a complete bike, combining the famous frame with the charismatic American engine seemed obvious – although accommodating the 45-degree V-twin required a bigger, stronger version of the Featherbed's steel tubes.

Goodman designed parts such as the fuel tank and seat on a computer, then had them constructed by local suppliers. Many components were built in-house, including the exhaust system, clip-on bars and adjustable footrests – plus the frame, which mounted the engine using rubber bushes to combat Harley's dreaded vibration. Other cycle parts came from Italy, notably the front end set-up of Marzocchi forks, floating Brembo discs and 18-inch magnesium wheel. Twin Koni shocks and Avon tyres completed the specification.

Harley contributed clocks, electrics and motor. Even when tuned with hotter camshafts and a larger 40mm carburetor, the pushrod V-twin produced only about 70bhp. But peak torque arrived at just 4000rpm, and the big black HDS gave plenty of grunt at half that figure.

Open the throttle at 40mph in top gear, and the Goodman charged forward with thrilling eagerness – and surprising smoothness, thanks to the rubber mounting. Firm suspension and well-chosen chassis dimensions gave handling that was excellent by Harley standards.

Typical Sportster vibration arrived at about 80mph, well short of the 120mph top speed, but for back-roads riding the Goodman was comfortable as well as respectably quick. Equally importantly the HDS was handsome and distinctive – a Harley hybrid in the best British cafe-racer tradition.

GOODMAN HDS1200 (1991)

Engine	Aircooled 4-valve pushrod 45-degree V-twin
Capacity	1200cc
Claimed power	70bhp at 5000rpm
Weight	204kg (450lbs) dry
Top speed	120mph (192km/h)
Standing quarter-mile	13.5sec/100mph (160km/h)

Left: The blend of US engine, Italian cycle-parts and British craftsmanship made a handsome bike.

Inset: The featherbed frame was enlarged to hold the Harley V-twin motor.

BIMOTA TESI 1D

Innovative, exotic and hugely expensive, Bimota's Tesi arrived in 1991 to lead motorcycling into the 21st century. The product of a decade's development by the world's most famous two-wheeled chassis specialists, the Tesi made history as the first series-production motorcycle to use hub-center steering instead of conventional front forks.

'Tesi' is the Italian word for thesis. The bike was so named because it was conceived for that purpose in the early Eighties by two Bologna University engineering students, who used Bimota's resources to build the first of several hub-center steered prototypes.

Separating a motorcycle's steering, braking and suspension forces should theoretically improve performance. But Tesi development was difficult, and stagnated until 1989 when Pierluigi Marconi, one of the former students, was appointed Bimota's chief engineer and revived the project.

The resultant roadster's 1D designation came from its Ducati engine, a watercooled V-twin from the 851. Either standard or tuned by Bimota with a long-stroke crankshaft that increased capacity to 904cc and peak power to 113bhp, the eight-valve desmo lump was particularly suitable because its stiff cases allowed a very light alloy frame.

A pair of horizontal aluminum arms ran from the frame to hold the 17-inch front wheel, which changed direction by pivoting on a bearing inside its hub. Handlebars were linked to the wheel by a series of rods. A near-horizontal mono-shock, similar to the rear unit, provided suspension.

In a straight line the radical bike felt deceptively normal,

thanks to its typically racy Bimota riding position and the characteristic delivery of the fuel-injected V-twin. In tuned form, the Ducati lump produced more midrange urge than ever, sending the Tesi storming to over 150mph. But it was the Bimota's handling that was remarkable. The way the Tesi's suspension continued to work, even with the front Brembos biting hard and the bike leaning deep into a corner, allowed unprecedented control.

Unfortunately, the original model proved very sensitive to adjustment of its Marzocchi suspension units and, unless correctly set up, gave an uneasy ride in bumpy bends. Switching to more sophisticated Ohlins units revealed the Tesi's full brilliance, supporting Marconi's belief that it represented the future of superbike design.

BIMOTA TESI ID (1991)	
Engine	Watercooled 8-valve DOHC desmodromic 90-degree V-twin
Capacity	904cc
Claimed power	113bhp at 8500rpm
Weight	188kg (414lbs) dry
Top speed	153mph (245km/h)
Standing quarter-mile	11.2sec/120mph (192km/h)

Above left: Hard cornering on the Tesi required a slight adjustment in riding style to allow for its differences from a conventional bike. Despite teething troubles, a correctly set-up Tesi inspired great confidence, offering distinct advantages when braking into a bend.

Above: Styling was far less radical than the chassis, but this was still one strange looking motorbike. High cost and motorcyclists' conservatism mean any revolution in front suspension design will be slow.

Left: This front-end shot shows how the horizontal alloy swing-arm works a shock absorber (upper right) via a linkage system.

TRIUMPH TRIDENT 900

At first glance Triumph's 900 Trident, a naked roadster with non-adjustable suspension and nostalgia-steeped British Racing Green paintwork, seemed too soft and simple to be much fun. One short ride was all the triple took to show how far that was from the truth.

What should have been the least interesting modular Triumph, the humble base-model Trident, turned out to be a revelation – at least in this long-stroke, 900cc form. (Triumph also made a short-stroke 750cc Trident.) Its blend of upright riding position, lively engine and nimble chassis provided as much excitement as almost anything on two wheels.

The key to the Trident's personality was its powerplant, basically three cylinders of the Trophy 1200 sports-tourer with an identical bottom-end. The watercooled, 12-valve engine produced a healthy 100bhp at 9500rpm, and its torque curve was every bit as flat as that of the bigger bike.

The motor was held in a steel spine frame identical to the Trophy's, though the naked bike's forks used softer springs and its shock was a cheaper unit from the same Japanese firm, Kayaba. The alloy swing-arm, twin-piston brakes,

wheels (17-inch front, 18-inch rear) and radial tires were common to both.

Styling was simple if slightly brutal, enhanced by classy deep-green paintwork. Like the other Triumphs the Trident was tall, and its raised bars and low footrests gave a roomy riding position that was ideal for gentle pottering – but which quickly became uncomfortable at speed. Handling was better than the specification suggested. The handlebars' width overcame conservative geometry to produce light, neutral steering. And the suspension worked reasonably well, despite lacking sophistication.

If the handling was responsive, it had nothing on the motor. The triple shared the 1200's seamless power delivery, pulling smoothly from 2000rpm to the 9500rpm redline. Crack open the throttle in first gear, and the front wheel leapt into the air. Roll it on in top, and the Triumph accelerated with magnificent authority toward a top speed of 135mph.

Like any unfaired bike, the Trident 900 was ill-suited to long trips or bad weather. But the rest of the time its simplicity, agility and boundless enthusiasm made a highly enjoyable combination.

TRIUMPH TRIDENT 900 (1991)	
Engine	Watercooled 12-valve DOHC transverse triple
Capacity	885cc
Claimed power	100bhp at 9500rpm
Weight	212kg (466lbs) dry
Top speed	135mph (216km/h)
Standing quarter-mile	12sec/117mph (187km/h)

Left: The responsive nature of the Trident's long-stroke engine made wheelies temptingly easy.

Below: Triumph's modular approach to design meant the naked 900 triple shared many components – including frame, forks, brakes and much of the engine – with the four-cylinder Trophy 1200.

Below left: Almost everyone who rode the 900 Trident agreed that its twin-cam motor was the best part of the bike. Short-stroke 750cc Trident was less impressive, although otherwise identical.

STORZ HARLEY-DAVIDSON XR883

It didn't look much like a sports bike, and it didn't look anything like a conventional race-replica. But one glance at the Storz XR883 was enough to inspire thoughts of racetrack glory, for this was a street-legal reproduction of the most famous competition motorcycle America has known.

Loud, lean and fast, the XR750 has been Harley-Davidson's factory dirt-track missile since 1972, winning countless races and numerous champions' No. 1 plates. Harley enthusiasts have converted ex-factory racebikes for the street, but, fittingly, it was former Milwaukee race mechanic Steve Storz who produced the ultimate roadgoing XR.

Storz prepared the machines that took Harley stars Ted Boody and Steve Morehead to top-four placings in the title race in the late Seventies, then left to start an accessory business near Los Angeles. His XR consisted of an 883 Sportster fitted with a kit that turned America's best-selling roadster into a facsimile of the nation's best-loved competition machine. Obvious modifications were the teardrop petrol tank, front mudguard and fiberglass tailpiece – all painted in Milwaukee's famous orange and black racing colors.

Harley's 883cc engine was internally standard but tuned with a 40mm Mikuni carburetor and a distinctive high-level exhaust. Suspension was uprated with 42mm Forcelle Italia forks in Storz yokes, Progressive Suspension shocks, and wider 18-inch wheels with a much-needed second front disc. The effect of the changes was obvious even at slow speeds, as the low, surprisingly light-feeling XR swapped the Sportster's laid-back slump for a semi-race crouch.

Even the 20 percent power increase did not lift the 45-degree V-twin's output much above 50bhp, but the raw, free-breathing XR pulled with distinctly improved response to a top speed approaching 120mph. And, although it was still more hog than gazelle, the taut and impressively agile Harley could be cornered and braked with confidence.

Steve Storz's XR883 roadster could never put its rider up front in the San Jose Mile, but it had the look.

Left: Storz bike's style was inspired by Harley's famous XR racers. Shotgun pipes (inset) gave a sporty look.

STORZ HARLEY-DAVIDSON XR883 (1991)

Engine	Aircooled 4-valve pushrod 45-degree V-twin
Capacity	883cc
Claimed power	55bhp at 5000rpm
Weight	200kg (440lbs) dry
Top speed	117mph (187km/h)
Standing quarter-mile	13.8sec/92mph (147km/h)

MOTO GUZZI DAYTONA 1000

Moto Guzzi's new sports bike was so long in development that cynics wondered whether the famous old firm from the banks of Lake Como, Italy, suffering from poor sales and lack of investment, would ever finish it. Finally, the Daytona was ready, and Guzzi's first superbike of the modern era proved well worth the wait.

Its American name was no coincidence. The Daytona was inspired and created by Dr John Wittner, a Philadelphia dentist-turned-tuner who had achieved great success, against the odds, with Guzzi-powered racebikes in the late Eighties. Delighted factory bosses invited Wittner to work on a road-going version, and the Daytona was the result.

Its engine was a tuned, 992cc version of Guzzi's trademark 90-degree transverse V-twin. Unlike the old pushrod Le Mans engine, the aircooled Daytona unit had a single overhead camshaft working four valves per cylinder. Fuel-injection helped lift output to a respectable 95bhp. The chassis was derived from Wittner's 'Dr John's' racebikes, and consisted of a steel spine frame, Marzocchi forks and a Koni monoshock whose layout incorporated a linkage to counteract the shaft drive's adverse effect on handling.

Styled with the assistance of Guzzi's huge wind tunnel, the Daytona was a handsome machine that retained the marque's unique character. Blipping the throttle at a standstill set the bike rocking in familiar fashion (a quirk of the cylinder arrangement); on the move, the engine's low-speed vibration disappeared in typical style to give a smooth ride.

Despite having slightly less of Guzzi's revered midrange torque, the Daytona was impressively flexible, its charge toward 150mph marred only by a typically notchy five-speed

Above: Guzzi's first sportster for the Nineties was fast, agile and handsome.

Right: Daytona's sleek styling was shaped in this huge wind-tunnel, built during the Fifties.

gearbox. Its long-legged feel and leant-forward riding position made for relaxed high-speed cruising. The combination of 17-inch front wheel, modern geometry and firm, well-damped suspension gave a sporty, flickable feel. The Daytona was stable at speed, too, and had powerful brakes and wide, sticky tires.

Even this heavily updated V-twin had neither the speed nor the agility of several lighter, more powerful and cheaper rivals, but the combination of Italian tradition and American flair had produced a uniquely enjoyable bike that looked set to lead Guzzi toward a more prosperous future.

MOTO GUZZI DAYTONA 1000 (1992)

Engine	Aircooled 8-valve SOHC 90-degree transverse V-twin
Capacity	992cc
Claimed power	95bhp at 8000rpm
Weight	205kg (451lbs) dry
Top speed	150mph (240km/h)
Standing quarter-mile	11.5sec/120mph (192km/h)

HONDA NR750

Depending on how it was viewed, Honda's exotic NR750 was either a visually and technically stunning superbike or an overweight, overpriced white elephant with unremarkable performance. One thing was certain: costing far more even than Bimota's Tesi, this was the most expensive roadster ever produced.

The NR owed its existence to the NR500 racebike with which Honda returned to grands prix in 1979. In an attempt to combat Yamaha and Suzuki's two-strokes with a four-stroke, they developed an oval-pistoned V4 engine that was the closest they could get to a V8. Despite spending billions of yen, Honda failed to make the 'Never Ready' competitive, and it was finally abandoned in 1981. But oval-pistoned

development continued, and 11 years later the NR750 was launched to recoup some prestige and profit.

Styling was as gorgeous as the NR's list of technical features was impressive. Its aggressive twin-headlamp fairing held a titanium-coated screen, below which was an innovative 'floating' LCD speedometer. The serpentine exhaust system's twin mufflers were set into a curvaceous, carbon-fiber reinforced tailpiece.

The chassis was fairly conventional, featuring a polished twin-beam alloy frame, Pro Arm single-sided swing-arm, thick 45mm upside-down forks, and a 16-inch front wheel. But there was nothing remotely ordinary about a water-cooled, 90-degree V4 containing pistons shaped like running

tracks, each with two conrods and eight tiny valves.

A peak output of 125bhp at 14,000rpm made the NR the world's most powerful 750, and the high-revving Honda had a wonderfully broad spread of torque. But despite extensive use of lightweight materials the NR weighed an excessive 488lbs. That meant its straight-line performance was no better than that of rival 750s costing a fraction of the price. Although the NR's rigid frame and top-quality cycle parts gave excellent handling, the seamless power delivery didn't make for a particularly exhilarating ride.

Regarded purely as a roadgoing motorcycle the NR750 was a disappointment, but to treat it that way was to miss the point. For all its drawbacks the NR was a motorcycling technological tour de force that perhaps only Honda, with their vast resources and obsession for superb precision engineering, could have produced.

HONDA NR750 (1992)

Engine	Watercooled 32-valve DOHC 90-degree V4
Capacity	748cc
Claimed power	125bhp at 14,000rpm
Weight	222kg (488lbs) dry
Top speed	158mph (253km/h)
Standing quarter-mile	11.2sec/123mph (197km/h)

Far left: A strong alloy frame and top-quality cycle parts made the NR a fine handler, despite its excessive weight.

Above: Gorgeous styling was a deliberate move away from conventional race-replica lines, with flowing curves and a host of exquisite details including titanium-coated screen and 'floating' instrument display.

Left: A serpentine exhaust system exited through the tailpiece. Rear wheel assembly included a single-sided swing-arm and predictably wide radial tire.

BARIGO 600 SUPER-MOTARD

Supermoto is a peculiarly French form of bike sport, half way between roadracing and motocross. Its mixture of asphalt and dirt track has led to the development of racebikes with high bars, powerful single-cylinder engines, long-travel suspension and fat roadrace tires, and also to a unique roadster: the Barigo 600.

Barigo is a small firm, run by former racer Patrick Barigault and based near La Rochelle in western France. Designed by Barigault and based on his successful supermoto championship racebike, the 600 combined locally-made parts with components from elsewhere in Europe. The Supermotard's engine was the latest watercooled big single from Austrian specialists Rotax. Fed by twin Dell'Orto carburetors and complete with twin cams, four valves and no fewer than three spark-plugs, it thumped out a claimed 61bhp at 8000rpm.

Barigo built the polished aluminum frame, to which were attached some classy cycle parts. Forks and shocks came from Dutch specialists White Power; brakes from Brembo. The 600's lightweight 17-inch magnesium wheels also originated in Italy, and wore fat Michelin sports bike radial tires.

If the Barigo's power output was remarkable for a single, its dry weight figure was amazing. The Supermotard scaled just 266lbs, far less than most big trail bikes and barely more than some 250cc machines. Combined with its wide bars, basic chassis rigidity, racy steering geometry and excellent multi-adjustable suspension, the Barigo's lack of weight made for a remarkably maneuverable bike. It could be flicked around effortlessly yet handled with great precision.

The Rotax motor was typical of a well-tuned big single, pulling hard at low engine speeds and vibrating noticeably, despite its balancer shaft, at higher revs. Although the 600 would cruise happily at 80mph with plenty in hand, the vibes and the upright riding position meant that speeds of over 100mph were best reserved for short bursts.

In its own way the Supermotard was every bit as single-minded as a conventional race-replica like Suzuki's GSX-R750. It certainly wasn't the ideal bike for everyone or every journey. But in town or on twisty backroads, the Barigo 600's blend of style, acceleration, agility, grip and braking power made it very hard to beat.

BARIGO 600 SUPERMOTARD (1992)

Engine	Watercooled 4-valve DOHC single
Capacity	598cc
Claimed power	61bhp at 8000rpm
Weight	121kg (266lbs) dry
Top speed	115mph (184km/h)
Standing quarter-mile	14sec/90mph (144km/h)

Left: Long-legged, torquey and impossibly light, the Barigo was essentially a supermoto racing machine.

DUCATI 888SPS

Fast red Ducatis were arguably *the* superbikes of the early Nineties, and the 888SPS was the greatest of them all. This was the 'Real Thing' – an exotic, exclusive and gloriously evocative recreation of the racebike that had made the World Superbike championship its own.

The SPS – short for Sport Production Special – was essentially a limited-edition version of the 888SP4, Ducati's 'normal' 1992 race-replica. The SP4 was powerful, light and expensive. The Special, of which only 100 examples were built,

was more powerful, lighter and several million lire more expensive still.

Both models used watercooled, 888cc V-twin engines and steel ladder frames based on those of Ducati's 851 roadster. Both had ultra-sophisticated Ohlins suspension units, carbon-fiber mudguards, streamlined single seats, Brembo Gold Line brakes and 17-inch wheels wearing fat, sticky Michelins. But the specification of the Special's eight-valve desmo engine was midway between that of the SP4 and Ducati's full-

DUCATI 888SPS (1992)	
Engine	Watercooled 8-valve DOHC desmodromic 90-degree V-twin
Capacity	888cc
Claimed power	120bhp at 10,500rpm
Weight	185kg (407lbs) dry
Top speed	160mph (256km/h)
Standing quarter-mile	11sec/122mph (195km/h)

Above: Designed as a street-legal racer, the SPS felt better the harder and faster it was ridden.

Right: Ducati equipped the 888 with a champion's No. 1 plate, as well as numerous chassis components made from lightweight carbon-fiber.

race powerplant. That meant bigger valves, racing camshafts, higher compression ratio, updated fuel-injection system, added fresh-air ducts – and a whopping rear-wheel output of 120bhp at 10,500rpm.

Chassis changes were aimed at shedding every unnecessary ounce. The SPS's petrol tank was made from carbon-fiber and Kevlar instead of steel. Exhaust mufflers and seat were also carbon, reducing weight to just 407lbs.

The resultant power-to-weight ratio ensured spectacular performance, particularly given the Ducati's predictable torrent of midrange torque. Even more memorable was the spine-tingling induction roar and the vibration that came hammering through the carbon-fiber tank, making full-bore

on the SPS a uniquely thrilling sensation.

Handling was as good as the Special's peerless pedigree suggested, though like a true racer the Ducati needed to be ridden aggressively. Treated gently it felt tall, cramped and slow-steering. But the harder and faster the SPS was cornered, the more its lightness and superb cycle parts proved their worth.

In a world of rapidly tightening legislation, the loud, raw and unashamedly racy 888SPS epitomized all that was exciting about modern sportsters, but it was too much motorcycle for many countries' power and emission limits even in 1992, and its days as a roadster were numbered. Few who rode the SPS would ever forget it.

SUZUKI GSX-R750W

Suzuki could hardly have dared hope, when they launched the GSX-R750 in 1985, that seven years later it would have gained a cult following and become established as the most popular race-replica of all. But the GSX-R's blend of speed, style and handling resulted in strong sales even when its impact on the world's racetracks had faded.

That success did not happen without plenty of effort. On the contrary, Suzuki worked tirelessly to improve the GSX-R – normally to good effect, in contrast to their troubles with the GSX-R1100. The result was that when in 1992 they finally abandoned the trademark oilcooling for watercooling, the GSX-R750W was merely another small step in a well-planned process of evolution.

The W was the third generation GSX-R, following the 1988 revision that had produced the 750J – better known as the Slingshot, after the name Suzuki coined for its carburetors. The Slingshot starred a stiffer frame with racier geometry, new suspension and 17-inch wheels, plus a shorter-stroke engine that increased power from 100 to 112bhp.

In fact the new bike was 40lbs heavier and barely faster than the original, but it had meatier midrange and delightfully light yet stable handling. Two years later the 750L raised the stakes again. Its return to original engine dimensions, combined with a reworked cylinder head and new exhaust, added power. Upside-down forks and fatter tires gave even sharper handling. Fine tuning of fairing, valvegear and frame geometry made 1991's 750M the best GSX-R yet, albeit by a tiny margin, but the need for more power and less width necessitated the introduction of the watercooled 750W some 12 months later.

Left: The GSX-R's sharp, race-hungry look changed little with the 750W model's adoption of a new watercooled engine.

Above: Always among the best-handling Japanese sportsters of all, the GSX-R became even more nimble over the years.

Numerous changes included a more compact engine that produced a claimed 116bhp, the highest yet, and was held lower and farther forward to put more weight on the front wheel. Frame dimensions and wheelbase were increased; steering geometry and swing-arm modified yet again.

Essentially the GSX-R750 had hardly changed at all. It was still fast and frenetic, agile and aggressive; a thrillingly crazy motorcycle at a sensible price. Naturally, it remained as popular as ever. Suzuki's policy of continual development had made sure of that.

SUZUKI GSX-R750W (1992)

Engine	Watercooled 16-valve DOHC transverse four
Capacity	749cc
Claimed power	116bhp at 11,500rpm
Weight	208kg (459lbs) dry
Top speed	154mph (246km/h)
Standing quarter-mile	11.2sec/122mph (195km/h)

LAVERDA 650

Laverda's fiery triples were among the greatest Seventies superbikes, but by the mid-Eighties sales had slumped and the firm from Breganze in northeastern Italy was on the brink of extinction. Salvation came when Laverda was taken over by the Zanini Group, a series of financial companies based in nearby Vicenza, in 1991.

Zanini invested big money to revive Laverda, and intensive development resulted in the launch, just a year later, of the 650. The comeback bike's engine could trace its history back to a mid-Seventies middleweight called the 500 Alpina, but the 650 was a far more sophisticated device.

The parallel twin motor was enlarged to 668cc, fitted with a new DOHC, eight-valve cylinder head and cooled by a mixture of oil and air. The gearbox and clutch were redesigned, and in place of carburetors the 650 used a Weber-Marelli fuel-injection system that helped boost peak power to 70bhp. The chassis was totally new, a typically modern layout comprising twin-beam aluminum frame, upside-down forks, rising-rate monoshock (both units supplied by Dutch specialists White Power), lightweight 17-inch wheels, big Brembo discs and low-profile Pirelli radial tires.

Complete with a sleek full fairing and single seat, the compact 650 scaled under 400lbs and carried its weight low thanks to an under-seat petrol tank. Steering was light and

Above: Light weight, a strong alloy twin-beam frame and top-notch White Power suspension gave the little 650 twin light and predictable handling.

Right: Sleek styling provided the 650 with an ultra-modern look, although Laverda's parallel twin motor had its origins way back in the Seventies.

neutral; the rigid frame and well-damped suspension gave excellent handling.

The Laverda felt flat at low revs but burst into action at 5500rpm, surging to 7500rpm and cruising smoothly at 100mph. Above that point the parallel twin's traditional vibration caused a buzz through the footpegs. If held flat-out, the Laverda would charge toward its 9500rpm redline and a top speed of over 130mph.

The 650's performance was mediocre by superbike standards; particularly by those of its illustrious predecessors. Rushed into production while bigger models – including a watercooled triple and even a roadgoing V6 – were developed, it was built in small numbers and expensive for a middleweight.

However, Laverda's bold new sportster was more than just promising – it was a handsome, fine-handling bike with a unique feel, and from a firm that had so recently seemed doomed, the 650 was proof of an amazing recovery.

LAVERDA 650 (1992)

Engine	Air/oilcooled 8-valve DOHC parallel twin
Capacity	668cc
Claimed power	70bhp at 8900rpm
Weight	180kg (396lbs) dry
Top speed	135mph (215km/h)
Standing quarter-mile	12sec/115mph (184km/h)

BIMOTA FURANO

Bimota hope that their revolutionary forkless Tesi will prove to be the future for superbike design, but in the meantime the Italian firm have produced some memorable conventional bikes, too. Several of these have combined Bimota's own twin-beam aluminum frame with the watercooled, four-cylinder engine from Yamaha's FZR1000.

Most lavishly equipped of all was the Furano. Hand-built in numbers of just 100, it added fuel-injection, lightweight carbon-fiber bodywork and top-of-the-range Ohlins suspension to an already mouth-watering specification. Yamaha's 1002cc FZR engine was left internally standard, but fed by Weber-Marelli injection instead of carburetors. The 20-valve motor breathed out through a four-into-one pipe of Bimota's own design, complete with carbon-fiber silencer. Claimed output was a monstrous – and some would say optimistic – 164bhp at 10,500 rpm.

No expense was spared in the chassis, which combined Bimota's aircraft alloy frame spars with Ohlins' sophisticated Swedish suspension parts. Lightweight materials, uncompromising design and high-quality construction resulted in minimal size and weight. The Furano shared its wheelbase and 396lbs weight figure with Yamaha's FZR600, rather than with the bigger FZR model.

It was finished to the standard for which Bimota had become renowned, meaning details like the monogrammed alloy top fork yoke, immaculate machining and welding, plus patches of carbon-fiber set into the fairing and seat/tank unit in a process so difficult that the factory claimed to reject one fairing in three.

Riding the Furano was a predictably sensational experience. The combination of awesome power, light weight and impeccably taut chassis gave a level of high-speed control that had to be experienced to be believed. Aim, brush the throttle and the Bimota was there – almost as though its controls were connected directly to your nervous system.

The Furano backed its neck-snapping acceleration with a top speed of over 170mph, and naturally it was rock-steady at whatever the velocity. But it was in slower bends that its race-track-firm suspension, huge Brembo brakes and sticky Michelin radials gave most advantage.

Like all Bimotas, the Furano was hideously expensive and totally impractical. The fortunate few who could afford one accepted that – for it was also arguably the fastest, most outrageous motorcycle money could buy.

BIMOTA FURANO (1992)

Engine	Watercooled 20-valve DOHC transverse four
Capacity	1002cc
Claimed power	164bhp at 10,500rpm
Weight	180kg (396lbs) dry
Top speed	172mph (275km/h)
Standing quarter-mile	10.7sec/129mph (206km/h)

Above left: Conventional in layout but not in its money-no-object use of materials, the Furano was the most powerful and exotic of all Bimota's Yamaha-engined roadsters.

Above: Few if any other superbikes could match the Furano's wonderfully taut feel in fast corners, where its hand-assembled chassis, classy Ohlins suspension and sticky Michelin radials came into their own.

Left: Tuned by Bimota with fuel-injection and a new exhaust system, Yamaha's fearsome FZR1000 motor was even more responsive than ever.

Inset: The FireBlade's remarkable lack of weight heralded a new era for mass-produced superbike design, and helped give the Honda superbly agile handling.

Below: Layout and styling were conventional race-replica stuff. At a standstill the 900RR looked rather ordinary, but riding it told a very different story.

HONDA CBR900RR FIREBLADE

For several years Honda held back from building a big-bore sportster, seemingly because they did not want to fuel the calls for legislation to limit performance. But in 1992, with a 100bhp limit looming nevertheless, Honda joined battle by unleashing a thrillingly sharp-edged superbike.

In marked contrast to the revolutionary NR750, they did so with a machine that had a conventional layout and contained little untried technology. Instead, the CBR900RR FireBlade relied for its speed on the old-fashioned combination of heavy horsepower and light weight.

Its motor was a watercooled, 16-valve four producing a maximum of 123bhp at 10,500rpm. The output was impressive, but Honda's real achievement was that the 893cc engine, crammed full of lightweight components, was barely bigger or heavier than their CBR600 powerplant.

The same was true of the FireBlade's chassis, which combined a twin-beam alloy frame with – more surprisingly – thick, 45mm forks that were not the fashionable upside-down variety, and which held a 16-inch front wheel instead of the 17-inch norm.

Every effort was made to make the CBR as light and maneuverable as possible. Its fairing contained a rash of small holes that were claimed to improve cornering performance by enhancing airflow. Steering geometry was racy; overall weight a mere 407lbs – comparable with a Japanese middleweight or hand-built Bimota.

Performance was predictably fearsome, although the CBR motor had slightly less midrange muscle than its heavier, more powerful FZR and GSX-R rivals. Instead, it combined smooth, high-revving response with razor-sharp handling, brilliant braking and generous grip from specially-developed Bridgestone radial tires.

The wonderfully quick-steering FireBlade could feel almost unstable at times but in most situations it was unbeatable, at least by a mass-produced motorcycle. Honda had raised the speed stakes yet again, and the 900 pilot's only problem was that the bike's performance could rarely be used to the full on public roads.

That was the inevitable result of changing technology, and a look back at the CBR900RR's ancestry was illuminating. Comparing the FireBlade with Honda's original, 1969-model CB750 – 56bhp less powerful, over 70lbs heavier and 40mph slower – revealed just how far superbikes had advanced in a little over two decades.

HONDA CBR900RR FIREBLADE (1992)

Engine	Watercooled 16-valve DOHC transverse four
Capacity	893cc
Claimed power	123bhp at 10,500rpm
Weight	185kg (407lbs) dry
Top speed	165mph (264km/h)
Standing quarter-mile	10.8sec/126mph (202km/h)

INDEX

ACKNOWLEDGMENTS

The author and publishers would like to thank Mike Rose for designing this book, Stephen Small for the picture research and Ron Watson for compiling the index. The following individuals supplied photographic material:

Roland Brown, pages: 14, 40-41(both), 65, 76, 79(both), 80, 81, 84-85(all three), 86-87(both), 88-89(both), 90-91(all three), 92-93, 93, 94-95(both), 96, 97, 100-101, 102, 102-103, 104, 105, 106, 108-109(all three), 110(inset).
Jack Burnicle, page: 10(inset).
Kel Edge, pages: 1, 2-3, 35, 47(bottom), 48(inset), 52-53, 56, 57, 62-63, 66, 68(inset), 72-73, 106-107.
David Goldman, pages: 4-5, 10-11, 22-23(both), 38-39, 39, 50, 51, 63, 64, 66-67, 68-69, 70-71, 71, 72, 73(bottom), 77(top), 78(both), 83(both), 110-111.
Roy Kidney, pages: 26-27.
Phil Masters, page: 34.
Mac McDiarmid, pages: 12, 13, 92, 98-99(all three).
Andrew Morland, pages: 6, 9(both), 18-19(all three), 20-21(both), 44-45(all three), 46.
Don Morley, pages: 8-9, 15(both), 16, 17, 24-25(both), 32-33(both), 37, 38(inset), 42-43(all three), 54-55, 58-59, 59(inset).
John Nutting, pages: 28-29(both), 30-31(both), 36, 47(top), 48-49.
Colin Schiller, pages: 52, 53(bottom), 60, 61.
Oli Tennant, pages: 7(both), 77(bottom), 82.